MARKETING BEYOND BORDERS
A Strategic Roadmap for SME Businesses

VIDYUT SHAH
MARKETING STRATEGIST

BLUEROSE PUBLISHERS
India | U.K.

Copyright © Vidyut Shah 2025

All rights reserved by author. No part of this publication may be reproduced, stored in a retrieval system or transmitted in any form or by any means, electronic, mechanical, photocopying, recording or otherwise, without the prior permission of the author. Although every precaution has been taken to verify the accuracy of the information contained herein, the publisher assumes no responsibility for any errors or omissions. No liability is assumed for damages that may result from the use of information contained within.

BlueRose Publishers takes no responsibility for any damages, losses, or liabilities that may arise from the use or misuse of the information, products, or services provided in this publication.

For permissions requests or inquiries regarding this publication, please contact:

BLUEROSE PUBLISHERS
www.BlueRoseONE.com
info@bluerosepublishers.com
+91 8882 898 898
+4407342408967

ISBN: 978-93-6783-156-4

First Edition: January 2025

MARKETING BEYOND BORDERS

A Strategic Roadmap for SME Businesses

Vidyut Shah

Marketing Strategist

A Part of Holistique Business Series

The world beyond borders is full of opportunities, but it's also fraught with challenges. Success comes to those who navigate both with equal skill.

TABLE OF CONTENT

Dedication	11
Acknowledgement	12
Preface	13
About The Book	18
Purpose Of The Book	21
A Word Of Caution For Readers	22
Foreword	23
About The Author	26
A Prelude	31
Part 1 - Across The Borders	35
Chapter 1: SMEs In Strategic International Marketing	36
• Objectives Of SME Businesses	39
• Goals Of SME Businesses	40
• Smart Goals Guiding The Way	42
Part 2: SMEs In Fore Front	44
Chapter 2: SMEs On Path To International Expansion	45
• Your Encounter With Pains	45
• Your Pains Have A Cure	47

Part 3: Enticing Anecdotes To Emulate — 50

Chapter 3: Draw Inspiration: Your Food For Thought — 51

- Marketing Beyond Borders - A Saga Of Aspirations And Ambitions — 51

Chapter 4: Cricket And International Marketing: A Winning Analogy — 55

Part 4: Foundation Of Strategic International Marketing — 59

Chapter 5: Nuances Of Strategic International Marketing — 60

- Strategic International Marketing - A Connotation — 60
- Emerging Key Elements — 61
- Critical Tasks Performed — 62
- Domestic and International Marketing: A Distinction — 63
- International and Global Marketing : A Distinction — 66
- International Vs Global Marketing: The Choice Criteria — 67

PART 5 Ringside View — 68

Chapter 6: Vistas Of International Marketing — 69
- Guard against Common Mistakes — 71
- Challenges of International Marketing — 72
- Key issues related to Language Barriers — 73
- Key Economic Challenges — 74
- Strategies to Combat Challenges — 74
- Overcoming Language Barriers — 75
- Navigating Economic Factors — 75

PART 6 Global Market Environment — 77

Chapter 7: Scanning The Environment — 78
- Market Categories — 78
- Economic Environment — 79
- Political Environment — 80
- Legal Environment — 81
- Cultural Environment — 81
- Technological Environment — 82

PART 7 Crafting an International Marketing Strategy — 83

Chapter 8: Strategic Framework — 84

- Fundamental Principles of International Marketing — 85
- A Range of 10 Relevant Questions — 86
- Role of Technology and Data-Driven Insights — 87
- Stages of International Marketing Strategy — 88
- Creation of A Strategic Roadmap — 91
- Target Market Selection — 93
- Competitive Analysis — 93
- Positioning and Differentiation — 94
- Product Strategy — 95
- Pricing Strategy — 95
- Promotion Strategy — 96
- Distribution and Logistics — 96
- Monitoring and Evaluation — 98
- Risk Management — 99
- Significance of Automation — 100
- Role of Cultural Sensitivity — 101
- Strategies for Implementing Cultural Sensitivity — 101
- Localisation — 102

PART 8 : A Strategic Fusion — 104

Chapter 9: Strategies Galore — 105

- Strategy 1: Market Research And Analysis — 108
- Strategy 2: Budgeting, Financial Planning And Risk Management — 116
- Strategy 3: Marketing- Mix Strategy — 125
- Strategy 4: Global Market Segmentation — 134
- Strategy 5: International Market Entry — 137
- Strategy 6: Product Adaptation And Development — 145
- Strategy 7: Marketing Communications And Branding — 150
- Strategy 8: Pricing Strategies — 154
- Strategy 9: Distribution Channels And Supply Chain Management — 168
- Strategy 10: Leveraging Digital Marketing — 174
- Strategy 11: Customer Relationship Management (CRM) — 182
- Strategy 12: KPIs And Performance Measurement — 195

Part 9 : Tactical Moves — 202

Chapter 10 3Ts Strategy — 203

Chapter 11: From Blunders To Brilliance: A Story Of Globe- Trotting — 209

Chapter 12: Real- Life Case Studies — 216

Part 10 Eye on Future — 222

Chapter 13: Looking Ahead : Emerging Future Trends — 223

Part 11 In Hindsight — 229

Chapter14: Key Takeaways — 230

Chapter 15: Your Checklist For Action — 233

Epilogue — 241

In Retrospect — 242

A Vote Of Thanks — 243

DEDICATION

I dedicate this Book to eidetic memory of my most revered

Late Parents

Shri Navinchandra Shah & Smt. Kantaben Shah

my lovely wife and companion

Chaula

Trinity of my Assets

Priya- Chanakya- Hrushita

my adorable, ever-smiling & angelic

Grand Daughter – **TANISHKA (Pari)**

ACKNOWLEDGEMENT

It is my sacred obligation to place on record the vital contribution made by my near and dear ones in the presentation of this Book.

At the outset, I take this opportunity to express my profound gratitude to my family led by wife Chaula, and including daughter Priya, son Chanakya and daughter-in law Hrushita for their utmost care and concern, as usual, during the time I was busy penning this Book.

Big charming smiles on the face of my granddaughter Tanishka (our darling Pari) inspired me not a little!

PREFACE

The business has witnessed a total metamorphosis of sorts in the past few decades. SME businesses with the vision and drive to go global have emerged on the international plane. The large multinational corporations no longer enjoy the domain exclusivity. The smallest enterprises have succeeded in reaching customers thousands of miles away. Such a paradigm shift can be attributed to:

- proliferation of digital technologies
- advancements in logistics
- rise of e-commerce

While the rewards of international marketing can be substantial, the path to success is fraught with complexities that can overwhelm even the most seasoned entrepreneurs.

The idea for this book emerged as I noticed a recurring theme: small businesses, despite their potential, often falter in the international arena due to a lack of strategic planning and an understanding of the unique dynamics of global markets.

The digital revolution and advancements in communication and logistics have significantly created the level playing field for all. It now allows the SME businesses to compete alongside industry giants. Yet, venturing into international markets requires more than just an ambition. It demands a strategic and informed approach.

Marketing Beyond Borders-A Strategic Roadmap for SMES Businesses was born out of a recognition of the unique challenges and incredible opportunities that small businesses face when expanding beyond their local borders.

This book is conceived with the understanding that the path to international success is both challenging and rewarding. It is a journey that requires strategic planning, cultural sensitivity, and relentless innovation.

As a Marketing Strategist for very close to five decades, I have witnessed first-hand the transformative power of a well-executed international marketing strategy.

This book aims to demystify the complexities of global expansion. It seeks to delineate a clear, actionable Strategic Roadmap for SME business owners ready to take the leap.

I have had the privilege of mentoring numerous entrepreneurs and small business owners. My hand- holding has helped them unlock their potential and achieve remarkable success. This book is a culmination of those experiences. It reflects the collective wisdom of many who have embarked on this journey.

Throughout this book, you will find a blend of practical advice and insight into real-world case studies.

These elements are designed to equip you with the knowledge and tools needed to navigate the diverse cultural, economic, and regulatory landscapes of international markets.

The book unlocks an array of ideas of how to:

- identify and evaluate potential markets
- tailor your marketing strategies to meet the unique needs of different regions
- build strong, sustainable relationships with international customers

This book is not just a guide; it is a roadmap designed to help you identify opportunities, mitigate risks, and create a robust strategy that aligns with your business goals.

The focus is not on theory alone. The application of strategic principles that have been tested and proven in the real world have been accorded due prominence.

Each chapter builds on the last, offering a comprehensive view of what it takes to succeed in international marketing.

It is my fervent hope that the strategies and insights shared within these pages will inspire and **empower you to think Beyond Borders**. You will definitely succeed and transform your SME business into a global player.

The most successful global businesses are those that approach new markets with respect, curiosity, and a willingness to adapt and learn. With this mind-set, your small business can thrive on the international stage.

Get set on a journey of discovery, innovation, and global growth.

Thank you for embarking on this journey with me.

Here's to your success in the exciting world of **Strategic International Marketing!**

"Globalisation is a powerful force for change, both for companies and the countries in which they operate. Companies that want to stay ahead must learn to compete in the global marketplace. For small businesses, international marketing is the key to unlocking growth and achieving sustainable success."

Philips Kotler

P. S: Pursuit of International Marketing is a serious job.

It deserves to be treated as such.

However, remember the old adage:

"All work and no play makes Jack a dull boy."

Honouring the underlying spirit of this adage I have penned the following Chapters in the Book:

- **Draw Inspiration - Your Food for Thought**
- **Cricket and International Marketing - A Winning Analogy**
- **From Blunders to Brilliance- A Story of Globe -Trotting**

Still, it's always prudent to remember:

"All play and no work makes Jack a mere toy"

So now, let's get on with serious study of important concepts and strategies presented in the book:

"Marketing Beyond Borders: A Strategic Roadmap for SME Businesses"

ABOUT THE BOOK

For Whom and For Whom Not

In the diverse landscape of international business, understanding the specific audience for whom this book is crafted is crucial.

This book **Marketing Beyond Borders-A Strategic Roadmap for SME Businesses** is tailored to meet the needs of a specific group of readers.

However, it is admitted and acknowledged that for other classes of audience it might not be as beneficial.

This Chapter will help you determine if this book aligns with your professional goals, aspirations and current business context.

Who is this Book Meant for?

1. Small Business Owners and Entrepreneurs

- **Ambitious Entrepreneurs:** Those eager to expand their businesses internationally and seeking practical strategies and insights.
- **Established Small Business Owners:** Business owners with a local presence looking to scale their operations to international markets.
- **Start-up Founders:** New business owners aiming to understand the complexities of international marketing from the ground up.

2. Marketing Professionals

- **Digital Marketers:** Professionals focused on leveraging digital channels for international growth.
- **Marketing Managers:** Those responsible for strategic marketing decisions and looking to enhance their knowledge of global marketing practices.
- **Consultants and Advisors:** Experts who guide small businesses and start-ups in their marketing endeavours.

3. Academics and Students

- **Business Students:** Undergraduate and Graduate
- **Students:** Studying international business, marketing, or entrepreneurship.
- **Researchers:** Individuals conducting research in the fields of international marketing and small business growth.

4. Investors and Stakeholders

- **Venture Capitalists and Investors:** Individuals or entities interested in understanding the strategic marketing approaches of small businesses expanding internationally.
- **Business Mentors and Coaches:** Professionals who mentor small business owners and entrepreneurs in their growth journey.

Who is this Book Not Meant for?

1. Large Corporations

- **Established Global Giants:** Corporations with well-established international presence and advanced marketing departments might find the strategies too basic for their needs.

- **Corporate Executives:** Senior executives from large enterprises might seek more complex and high-level strategic insights than what is covered here.

2. Non-Business Readers

- **General Audience:** Individuals with no interest or involvement in business, marketing, or entrepreneurship.

- **Casual Readers:** Those looking for light reading or non-professional content might not find this book engaging.

3. Industry-Specific Professionals

- **Niche Market Professionals:** Professionals from highly specialised industries like, - medical devices, and aerospace requiring tailored marketing strategies are beyond the scope of this book.

- **Local Market Experts:** Those focused solely on local or domestic market strategies without any inclination towards international expansion.

My Submission, therefore is:

"**Marketing Beyond Borders - A Strategic Roadmap for SME Businesses**"is a comprehensive guide designed to empower SME business owners, entrepreneurs, marketing professionals, academics, and investors with the knowledge and tools needed for successful international expansion. It is they who will benefit the most.

For those outside this scope, there are numerous other resources better suited to their needs and interests.

PURPOSE OF THE BOOK

The purpose of this book is to demystify the complexities of international marketing and demonstrate its critical importance for SMEs.

Strategic international marketing enables SMEs to:

- diversify their customer base
- mitigate risks associated with economic fluctuations
- capitalise on opportunities in emerging markets

I am quite confident that SMEs can :

- achieve significant growth
- enhance brand recognition
- establish a strong global presence by mastering marketing strategies

A WORD OF CAUTION FOR READERS

Given the nature of this subject, you will encounter the terms "international," "marketing," and "strategies" frequently throughout the book.

While this repetition is unavoidable due to the core focus of our content, we assure you that each instance is purposeful and integral to the depth and clarity of the topics discussed.

Our aim is to provide you with a comprehensive understanding of the principles and practices that drive successful international marketing.

We have meticulously curated informative and relevant content to sustain your interest and enhance your learning experience. We encourage you to view these repeated terms not as monotonous, but as essential building blocks that reinforce key concepts and facilitate a cohesive narrative.

Thank you for your understanding and dedication. We hope you find the insights within these pages both enlightening and invaluable.

Cheers!

FOREWORD

In an era where the world is more connected than ever before, the ability of small businesses to compete on a global scale has been significantly enhanced. The barriers that once limited small enterprises to local markets are now overshadowed by unprecedented opportunities for international growth and expansion. However, with these opportunities come unique and concomitant challenges that require strategic insight, cultural understanding, and innovative marketing approaches.

The book "**Marketing Beyond Borders- A Strategic Roadmap for SME Businesses**" arrives at a pivotal moment in the global economy. As a business professional who has spent years navigating the intricacies of international markets, I have witnessed and realised the immense potential that lies in strategic global expansion. This book is a beacon for small business owners, particularly, in the SME sector who aspire to extend their reach beyond local borders and make a mark on the world stage!

The author, Vidyut Shah, brings a wealth of knowledge and experience to this topic. As a seasoned Marketing Strategist, he commands a deep understanding of the nuances involved in international marketing.

Practical approach of Vidyut Shah, coupled with a profound respect for cultural diversity, makes this book an invaluable resource for any SME looking to expand beyond borders.

What sets this book apart is its focus on basic concepts and actionable strategies tailored specifically for SMEs. While large corporations often have vast resources at their disposal, small businesses must rely on agility, creativity, and strategic planning to succeed.

Vidyut Shah has masterfully addressed these aspects, providing a clear Strategic Roadmap that SME owners can follow to achieve international success.

Throughout the pages of this book, readers will find a blend of insightful analysis, real-world examples, and expert advice. These elements come together to form a comprehensive guide that demystifies the complexities of international marketing. The strategies outlined here are not just theoretical concepts. But they contain practical tools, which, if used, can be implemented to achieve tangible results.

In a global market that is constantly evolving, staying ahead of the curve is crucial!

The book equips readers with the knowledge and skills needed to navigate this dynamic landscape. It encourages SME business owners to think globally, act locally, and embrace the rich diversity of international markets.

In other words, resort to **Marketing Beyond Borders.**

I am confident that this book will inspire and empower small business owners to take bold steps towards global expansion.

It is a testament to the author's expertise and passion for helping businesses succeed on an international scale.

As you embark on this journey, remember that the world is full of opportunities waiting to be explored. With the right strategies in place, your small business can achieve remarkable success and make a lasting impact on the global stage.

Warm regards,

Rahul Narvekar
Founder CEO : India Network
Ex-Founder NDTV Indianroots
Co-Founder Fashion and You
GP : Scale Ventures Fund

ABOUT THE AUTHOR

This is the first book written by my father Vidyut Shah after being pushed by his kids – me Priya Shah, his daughter; and my brother Chanakya - to pursue his love for writing and share his knowledge and experience with people for whom it's relevant and could be useful.

Deviating from normal convention, while my Father Vidyut Shah penned down this book, I snatched from him the opportunity to introduce himself.

Incidentally, I too have inherited flair for writing both from him as also my grandfather who was a Journalist of repute. Before I get down to pen down this column of About the Author, I must confess this is my modest attempt at introducing my Papa- my hero, my pride !

A 74 year young man, born in Ahmedabad, moved to Mumbai in childhood for 10 years with the family.

Ultimately from Ahmedabad, he came to Delhi at the age of 14. He continues to stay here till date and anytime hereafter.

This is tracing the journey of a brilliant Gujarati boy scoring well in Gujarat, labeled as a "dud" in Delhi owing to lack of knowledge of English language. He struggled and took up the challenge to prove his mettle in Delhi as a student. Relentless studies for more than 16 hours a day to cover up and be at par with all students became his sole motto.

In the process, Vidyut Shah almost lost eyesight in the bargain. But he came out with flying colors in the end. This is how a happy –go- lucky boy became a serious student winning laurels from everywhere.

The same habit continued and helped him win Gold Medal in the All -India Essay Competition on the topic of "Recession in India" at age of 17. This made him a star student. He pursued studies for B. A.(Hons) Economics from SRCC, Masters in Economics from Delhi School of Economics, University of Delhi. He then added further Post- Graduate Diploma in Marketing & Sales Management to hone his skills. He also holds a Diploma in French Language from Alliance Francaises.

Passion for writing led Vidyut Shah to produce and edit at the young age of 18 years, two magazines- one on Gujarat Development and the other on Export Performance.

Vidyut Shah took up the first job assignment in the Executive cadre at the premier International Trading Company of Government of India (Categorised as Mini Navratna Company) Total dedication, perseverance and trait of eye for detail, well- synchronised with the knowledge of Economics and Marketing, helped him achieve a prestigious position in the organisational ladder.

Excellent professional handling of varying facets of International Marketing encompassing Exports, Imports, Shipping and Transport, and Distribution earned Vidyut Shah the highest approbation from the company management.

Content Creation skill of Vidyut Shah was extensively deployed by his company in image building articles, event such as Gold Jewellery exhibition in Kuwait or Workshops and Seminars at home.

Vidyut Shah has excelled in handling some of the major items of Exports and Import. To name the few, they, inter alia, included Export of Basmati Rice, Processed Foods, Gold Jewellery, Readymade Garments, Leather wares and Distribution and Shipping of Edible Oils, Newsprint, Chemicals and Pharmaceuticals

Vidyut Shah had a rare privilege of being entrusted with a challenging Deputation assignment of 3 months to Paris and Francophone Countries.

Extensive overseas travel for work has been a significant landmark of his career. After putting in 17 years of Service, he secured Voluntary Retirement at the young age of 40.

It really requires guts to give up such a lucrative, cushy and secured job in such a young age ignoring bright future prospects. That is Vidyut Shah for you! - who loves challenges and creates his own individual path to progress.

Thereafter, he headed a couple of private and public limited companies in the CXO position to create and lead their exports business.

Now the family uses his knowledge for all the Marketing - Digital and Traditional - to grow the companies under his Chairmanship.

An ardent Cricket Fan, Vidyut Shah has great fancy for Music, Stand-up Comedy and Mimicry show. He is a family man to the core. His warm hospitality and event management skills and large- hearted compassion have always been a matter of admiration and adulation. His warm love and zeal for his only granddaughter is really commendable!

Wrapping up, perhaps my father couldn't find a better writer to take on legacy, it seems!

A PRELUDE

"Marketing across borders is like sailing unchartered seas- those who navigate with insight will find new words of opportunity."

A PRELUDE

Embarking on the journey of international marketing requires a well-crafted strategy. It should be both comprehensive and adaptable. Such a strategy must be grounded in comprehensive market research, cultural understanding, and a keen awareness of the global competitive landscape.

As businesses, especially SMEs, prepare to venture into international markets, they must:

- Conduct an in-depth market research
- Understand cultural nuances
- Assess legal and regulatory requirements
- Develop a robust entry strategy
- Leverage technology and innovation
- Build a strong local presence
- Monitor and adapt

Businesses can unlock new avenues for growth, resilience, and global success by embracing the vast opportunities of international marketing and crafting a strategic approach.

The path to becoming a global powerhouse starts with a bold vision and a meticulously planned strategy. Sustained excellence and innovation are the essential pre-requisites for success in the international arena.

In today's interconnected world, the boundaries that once confined businesses to local markets have dissolved. It has paved the way for unprecedented opportunities in the global marketplace.

For SMEs this paradigm shift presents both a challenge and an exciting prospect.

The allure of international markets lies in its vast potential for revenue growth. Further, the rich diversity of consumer needs and preferences are more than tempting for any effort.

This book," **Marketing Beyond Borders - A Strategic Roadmap for SME Businesses**" is designed to be your comprehensive guide to navigating the complexities of global expansion. Whether you're a seasoned entrepreneur looking to expand your horizons or a budding business owner eager to tap into international markets, this book will arm you with the insights, strategies, and tools so necessary for success.

We'll explore how small businesses can leverage their inherent agility to:

- adapt to different cultural landscapes
- develop tailored marketing strategies
- build strong, lasting relationships with international customers.

By the end of this journey, you'll be well-prepared to take your small business Beyond Borders and achieve remarkable growth in the global arena.

To substantiate the role and importance of SME Businesses on international plane, relevant and authentic statistics speak volumes:

SMEs contribute approximately

- 45% of the total employment
- around 50% of the global GDP
- 35% of global exports

Digital Presence

75% of SMEs with a strong digital presence are more likely to engage in international markets.(OECD Study-2023)

Challenges in International Markets

- 62% of SMEs cite regulatory challenges as a significant barrier to international trade(World Bank Survey)

SME Contribution to Exports

- SMEs in India contribute about 48% of the country's total exports.
- The Indian government aims to increase this contribution to 60% by 2025.

Digital Adoption

- 58% of Indian SMEs using digital marketing tools have expanded into international markets.(CII Report-2022)

Growth Rate

- The Indian SME sector has been growing at a rate of 10% per annum.

- Majority of enterprises are tapping into international markets, especially in sectors like textiles, IT, and pharmaceuticals.

Government Initiative

Government initiatives like **Make in India** and **MSME Champions** have provided support to around 6,000 Indian SMEs to enter international markets between 2020-2023.

Challenges and Opportunities

Cost Barriers

50% of SMEs report that high costs related to international marketing -such as compliance and logistics- are a major hurdle to entering global market.

Market Diversification

60% of SMEs globally are looking to diversify their markets beyond their domestic regions, with Asia and Africa emerging as key regions of interest. (HSBC Report-2022)

These statistics illustrate in ample measure the growing role of SMEs in international markets, highlighting both the opportunities and challenges they face in expanding their global reach.

PART 1
ACROSS THE BORDERS

"To be successful in the global marketplace, it's critical to have a deep understanding of the local context and culture. We don't just sell technology; we empower every country, every organisation, and every person to achieve more in their own unique way."

- Satya Nadella, CEO of Microsoft

CHAPTER 1

SMEs IN STRATEGIC INTERNATIONAL MARKETING

Unlock new revenue streams—find out how international marketing can transform your small business.

Strategic international marketing is crucial for SME businesses. Entry of SME businesses on an international plane is justified for more than one reason as it dishes out a number of **benefits**.

1. **Expansion of Market Reach**

- **Access to New Markets:** Small businesses can expand their customer base by entering international markets to achieve increased sales and revenue.

- **Diversification of Revenue Streams:** Risks associated with economic downturns encountered by the small businesses in the home country can be mitigated by overcoming their sole dependance on the domestic market.

2. **Enhanced Brand Recognition and Reputation**

- **Global Brand Presence:** Entry into international markets can enhance brand visibility and reputation.

- **Competitive Advantage:** The SME businesses can gain a strong competitive advantage vis-a-vis their competitors operating only in the domestic market.

3. Economic Benefits

- **Economies of Scale:** By scaling up production to cater to international demand, SME businesses can achieve cost efficiencies.
- **Increased Profits:** Gaining access to markets with higher purchasing power, SME businesses succeed in earning higher profit margins.

4. Innovation and Learning

- **Exposure to New Ideas:** SME businesses become familiar with different customer preferences leading to the rise of innovation in their package of products and services.
- **Learning Opportunities:** Participation in international operations affords valuable insights to SME businesses into business practices and market trends.

5. Improved Business Resilience

- **Risk Management:** SME businesses are able to effectively gear up to withstand local economic fluctuations and political instability by diversifying markets.

- **Sustainability:** A diversified market portfolio ensures a more stable revenue stream for the SME businesses contributing to their long-term sustainability.

6. Access to Talent and Resources

- **Global Talent Pool:** International operations can attract a diverse talent pool, bringing in diverse skills and perspectives.

- **Resource Optimisation:** Resource availability and cost-effectiveness get a boost by access to international suppliers and partners.

7. Technological Advancements

- **Adoption of Technology:** Competing internationally entails adoption of the latest technologies for communication, production, and marketing.

- **Digital Marketing:** Leveraging digital marketing tools can enhance prospects of global reach with cost-effective methods.

8. Regulatory and Policy

- **Regulatory and Policy Benefits:** SME businesses can benefit from favourable trade agreements between their home country and others, which can reduce tariffs and ease market entry.

- **Government Support:** The SME businesses can avail of support and incentives offered by many governments to expand internationally.

9. Customer Base Diversification

- **Targeted Marketing:** International markets provide opportunities in altogether new niche segments that may not exist in the domestic market.

- **Cultural Adaptation:** Understanding and adapting to different cultures can improve prospects of delivering products and services to a broader audience.

10. Partnership and Networking Opportunities

- **Strategic Alliances:** Forging strategic partnerships with international companies can facilitate mutual growth and access to new market opportunities.

David Abney, former CEO of UPS, stated:

"For small businesses, strategic international marketing is not just an opportunity; it's a critical pathway to growth and innovation. By leveraging global markets, small businesses can find new customers, learn from diverse markets, and build a robust foundation for long-term success. In today's interconnected world, those who think globally will lead locally."

This quote highlights how strategic international marketing is essential for small businesses to grow, innovate, and succeed in a globalised economy.

Objectives of SME Businesses

SMEs enter international arena of marketing with a set of objectives and goals:

- **Market Expansion:** Identify and enter new international markets to increase the customer base and revenue streams.

- **Brand Awareness:** Establish and enhance brand recognition and reputation in foreign markets.

- **Competitive Advantage:** Develop a unique value proposition to differentiate from local and international competitors.

- **Customer Acquisition and Retention:** Acquire new customers and maintain existing ones through targeted marketing strategies and customer relationship management.

- **Adaptation and Localisation:** Adapt products, services, and marketing strategies to meet the cultural, legal, and consumer preferences of the international markets.

- **Risk Diversification:** Spread business risks by not relying solely on domestic markets.

- **Innovation and Learning:** Leverage international experiences to innovate and improve products, services, and business processes.

Goals of SME Businesses

- **Revenue Growth:** Achieve specific sales targets and revenue growth in the international markets within a defined timeframe.

- **Market Penetration:** Attain a certain percentage of market share in the target international markets.

- **Customer Satisfaction:** Reach high levels of customer satisfaction and loyalty through quality products, services, and customer support.

- **Brand Positioning:** Position the brand as a leader or a significant player in the international market segments targeted.

- **Cost Efficiency:** Optimise marketing expenditures and achieve a high return on investment (ROI) for international marketing campaigns.

- **Regulatory Compliance:** Ensure full compliance with international trade regulations, local laws, and industry standards in all target markets.

- **Sustainable Growth:** Foster long-term, sustainable business growth by building strong relationships with international partners, suppliers, and customers.

- **Innovation:** Introduce new products or services tailored to the needs and preferences of the international market.

SMART GOALS

SMART Goals Guiding the Way

Devising SMART Goals Strategy for success is sine qua non for success in any field and international marketing is no exception!

- **Specific:** Goals should be specific and well-defined so that achievable plans can be developed.

- **Measurable:** Use quantifiable metrics -sales volumes, market share, customer acquisition or brand awareness.

- **Achievable:** Consider factors such as market conditions, competition, and capabilities of companies to set achievable goals.

- **Relevant:** Ensure that international marketing goals support the mission, vision and core values of the company.

- **Time Bound:** Set a clear timeframe and deadline to create a sense of urgency.

Wrapping Up

Successfully navigating strategic international marketing allows small businesses to tap into new markets and gain a competitive edge.

By tailoring strategies to specific international audiences, they can create sustainable growth opportunities and enhance brand visibility globally.

PART 2
SMEs IN FOREFRONT

Understanding and respecting cultural differences is the cornerstone of success in global markets. At PepsiCo, we didn't just adapt our products to different markets—we immersed ourselves in the local culture to become a part of it, creating a strong emotional connection with our global consumers."

- Indra Nooyi, Former CEO of PepsiCo

CHAPTER 2

SMEs ON PATH TO INTERNATIONAL EXPANSION

Struggling with stagnant growth? International markets could be your next big move!

Your Encounter with Pains

As owners of SME businesses, are you struggling with a range of pains relating to a variety of issues while undertaking Strategic International Marketing?

Your Pains are quite palpable as I can see them

- Lack of understanding of cultural, economic, and legal differences in foreign markets.
- Difficulty in complying with international regulations and standards.
- Fluctuating currency exchange rates and financial instability.
- Ineffectiveness of one-size-fits-all marketing strategies.
- Building brand awareness in new and competitive markets.
- Complexities in managing international logistics and supply chains.
- Language barriers and miscommunication with foreign clients and partners.
- Difficulty in executing effective digital marketing campaigns across different countries.
- Establishing credibility and trust with a new customer base.
- Identifying and managing reliable international partners and distributors.
- Setting competitive yet profitable pricing in diverse markets.
- Protecting intellectual property in foreign markets.

- Navigating cultural sensitivities and ethical considerations.
- Limited resources to scale operations internationally.
- Adapting to different technological landscapes and consumer behaviours.

But Your Pains Have A Cure

A strong will to scale up on an international plane, makes the SME business owner undaunted and unruffled. He is determined to Cure the Pains and move on.

A Strategic Road map is created for embarking on the International Stage.

In the world of business, the journey of **Marketing Beyond Borders** starts.

This leap is driven by a mind-set of growth, resilience, and unwavering ambition.

The ability to navigate different cultures, understand diverse markets, and build global relationships is of paramount importance.

Entering international markets requires more than just a business plan.

It demands a specific Mindset characterised by:

- **Adaptability:** The willingness to embrace change and adapt strategies to fit into new and varied markets.

- **Resilience:** The strength to overcome challenges and setbacks, viewing them as opportunities for learning and growth.
- **Vision:** A clear and compelling vision of what can be achieved on an international scale.
- **Openness:** An openness to new ideas, perspectives, and ways of doing business, recognising the role of innovative approaches in the realm of international marketing.
- **Commitment to Quality:** Maintaining the high standards of every new market, tolerating no compromise on quality.

For Business Owners the journey to international markets is primarily about:

- business expansion
- ambition fulfilment
- making a mark on the world stage
- bringing unique offerings to a broader audience
- fostering cross-cultural connections
- contributing to the global economy

In a way, it is an aspiration to create a legacy of excellence, innovation, and trust that transcends borders.

These ideas capture the essence of the role, importance, and mind-set of SME business owners preparing for international marketing, highlighting the qualities that will drive their success on the global stage.

A gamut of conceptual framework and an amalgam of diverse Marketing Strategies drawn up in succeeding pages shall ,and hopefully will, guide the efforts of SME business owners to ultimate success on an international plane.

Wrapping Up

International expansion offers small businesses the chance to diversify their revenue streams and reduce dependence on local markets.

Careful planning and market research are essential to overcoming challenges and seizing the opportunities that global markets present.

PART 3
ENTICING ANECDOTES TO EMULATE

"When Starbucks entered international markets, we knew we had to maintain the authenticity of our brand while also adapting to local tastes and preferences. This balance between consistency and customisation has been key to our global success."

- Howard Schultz, Former CEO of Starbucks

CHAPTER 3

DRAW INSPIRATION: YOUR FOOD FOR THOUGHT

Unlock new revenue streams—find out how international marketing can transform your small business.

Marketing Beyond Borders - A Saga of Aspirations and Ambitions

At the outset, I would like to share an enchanting story of a Small Businessman.

Here, unfolds a Journey of Resilience and an inspiring story of Raj Patel and his Handicrafts Business .

Raj Patel, a small business owner from a rural village in Mehsana district of Gujarat, India had a dream to take his family's traditional Handicraft business to the terrains of the international market.

His journey testifies the power of resilience, passion and human spirit in the face of challenges.

Modest beginnings

Raj grew up watching his parents and grandparents meticulously create beautiful handcrafted items from wood, metal, and clay. Their products were well-known in local markets.

However, Raj had bigger dreams. He wanted to share the unique craftsmanship of his village with the world.

Overcoming Challenges

Raj's ensuing journey was far from easy. The first major hurdle related to finance. With limited resources, he needed to find a way to market his products internationally.

Raj attended numerous workshops and training sessions on international marketing. He was busy learning about export regulations, pricing strategies, and cultural differences in consumer behaviour.

Building Relationships

One of Raj's key strategies was building strong relationships. He traveled to international trade fairs, a venue where he met potential buyers and partners.

Raj's genuine passion for his craft and his respectful, humble approach won him many friends and supporters. He often invited these new friends to his village. He started showing them the process of creating each handicraft item. He built up personal connections that went beyond business.

Embracing Digital Marketing

Raj realised the potential of digital marketing. With the help of a local friend, he set up a website and social media profiles for his business. Raj shared stories of his artisans, highlighting their skills and the cultural significance of their work. His transparency and the authentic narrative attracted a loyal customer base from around the world.

Grand Success

Today, Raj's business exports handicrafts to over 15 countries. His success has transformed his village, providing employment to over 200 artisans and improving the local economy.

Giving back to community

But Raj's story doesn't end with his business success. He established a training centre in his village, where young people learn the art of handicraft and the skills needed for international marketing.

Raj's vision is not just to expand his business, but to uplift his entire community.

Lessons Learned

Raj Patel's story teaches us that, no doubt, international marketing is about strategies and techniques. It is much more.

It's about people, relationships, and the passion behind a product. His journey is a powerful reminder that small businesses, with the right approach, can achieve great success on an international platform.

CHAPTER 4

CRICKET AND INTERNATIONAL MARKETING: A WINNING ANALOGY

The clock is ticking—take advantage of global opportunities before your competition does!

Cricket in India is nothing short of a national religion.

Annexing the T20 World Cup in West Indies on 29th June, 2024, after defeating South Africa was an icing on the cake for the Cricket enthusiasts all over India. Their joy and jubilation almost touched the sky! (SKY for Surya Kumar Yadav).

Just like in cricket, achieving success in strategic international marketing for small businesses requires total dedication, devotion, and team spirit.

Imagine your marketing team as the Indian cricket team, gearing up for the World Cup Final.

Here's how the roles and strategies align perfectly:

1. Captain (CEO/CMO)

The captain of the cricket team is like the CEO or CMO of your business. He needs to have a clear vision, make strategic decisions, and inspire the team to perform at their best.

Just as Rohit Sharma led India to World Cup victory with his cool-headed strategies, your CEO should lead the marketing team with confidence and foresight.

2. Opening Batsmen (Initial Market Entry)

The opening batsmen face the first deliveries and set the tone for the rest of the innings. Similarly, your initial market entry strategy needs to be strong and well-prepared. It's about making a solid first impression and laying the groundwork for future success.

Remember, Virender Sehwag of yesteryears or now Rohit Sharma -like their explosive start can give you an early advantage!

3. Middle Order Batsmen (Brand Building)

The middle-order batsmen stabilise the innings and build on the foundation set by the openers.

In marketing, this is your brand-building phase.

Consistency is key, much like that of Rahul Dravid in the recent past or Rohit- Kohli combination of dependable batting. Establishing your brand's credibility and connecting with your audience steadily will ensure a strong position in the market.

4. All-Rounders (Versatile Marketing Strategies)

All-rounders are the adaptable players who can bat, bowl, and field. In international marketing, you need versatile strategies that cover all bases – social media, content marketing, SEO, and more. Think of your marketing team as having the versatility of Ravindra Jadeja or Hardik Pandya always ready to tackle any challenge head-on.

5. Bowlers (Targeted Campaigns)

Just as bowlers aim to take wickets with precise deliveries -good length and yokers- your targeted marketing campaigns should aim to capture leads and convert them into customers.

A lethal mix of Pace and Spin, like that of Jasprit Bumrah and Kuldeep Yadav can keep your competitors guessing and your audience engaged.

6. Fielders (Customer Support)

Fielders save runs and take catches, just like excellent customer support saves clients and wins over sceptics.

A well-fielded marketing campaign can turn potential disasters into opportunities, much like a stunning catch by Surya Kumar Yadav in the last over of the unforgettable Final Match!

7. Coach (Marketing Consultant): Behind every great team is a great coach.

Your marketing consultant plays a similar role, offering guidance, strategy, and expertise. He helps the team refine their techniques and improve performance, just as old veteran ,Rahul Dravid , Mr Wall as popularly known , did for Team India.

Lesson learnt

In the game of Cricket and Strategic International Marketing, the synergy of a dedicated team, strategic planning, and adaptable tactics leads to success.

So, gear up, plan your innings, and knock those marketing challenges out of the park!

And remember, just like the World Cup victory, celebrating your marketing milestones will make the journey enjoyable for everyone involved.

Say, hip hip hooray!!!

PART 4
FOUNDATION OF STRATEGIC INTERNATIONAL MARKETING

"Going global isn't about imposing your ideas on new markets; it's about listening, learning, and adapting. At Virgin, we've always embraced the differences that make each market unique, which has allowed us to build businesses that resonate with people across the world."

- Richard Branson, Founder of Virgin Group

CHAPTER 5
NUANCES OF STRATEGIC INTERNATIONAL MARKETING

The world is your market—start your small business's global journey today!

Strategic International Marketing : A Connotation

Strategic International Marketing refers to the systematic planning, development, and execution of marketing strategies that are tailored to target audiences in multiple countries. It involves:

- analysis of foreign markets
- understanding of cultural differences
- adapting marketing efforts to meet the specific needs
- preferences of international consumers

This approach aims to:

- achieve competitive advantage
- secure business growth by leveraging opportunities across global markets

In the words of Philip Kotler, the Father of Marketing Management - Strategic International Marketing is:

"The process of identifying and pursuing opportunities in international markets through coordinated, carefully planned activities that encompass market research, product development, promotion, distribution, and pricing strategies. It involves a comprehensive understanding of cultural, economic, and regulatory differences to effectively position and sell products or services globally."

Emerging Key Elements

1. **Market Research:** Collection and analysis of data about foreign markets to understand customer needs, market trends, and competitive landscapes.

2. **Cultural Sensitivity:** Adapting marketing messages and tactics to align with the cultural norms and values of target markets.

3. **Product Development:** By modifying products or services, meet the unique requirements and preferences of international customers.

4. **Promotion:** Creation and implementation of promotional campaigns that resonate with local audiences and comply with regional regulations.

5. **Distribution:** Establishment of efficient distribution channels to ensure products are available and accessible in target markets.

6. **Pricing Strategy:** Setting prices reflecting local economic conditions, purchasing power, and competitive pricing structures.

Critical Tasks Performed

International marketing performs critical tasks to:

- explore new markets
- increase its customer base
- create and improve brand awareness
- create revenue stream

Domestic and International Marketing: A Distinction

The distinction between domestic and international marketing is accounted for by the scope, environment, and strategies employed to reach the target market.

Points of key distinction are:

1. Scope and Reach

Domestic Marketing: Focuses on a single market, typically within the marketer's home country. The target audience shares similar cultural, economic, and legal environments.

International Marketing: Involves marketing products or services in multiple countries. It requires understanding and adapting to diverse cultural, economic, and legal environments.

2. Cultural Differences

Domestic Marketing: Cultural homogeneity makes it easier to create marketing messages that resonate with the entire target audience.

International Marketing: Cultural diversity requires tailoring marketing strategies to fit local customs, traditions, and consumer behaviours. This can include adjusting product offerings, branding, and communication styles.

3. Economic Environment

Domestic Marketing: Operates within a single economic system, making it easier to predict market trends and consumer behaviour.

International Marketing: Must navigate varying economic conditions, including differences in currency, purchasing power, and economic stability. This can affect pricing, distribution, and promotional strategies.

4. Legal and Regulatory Framework

Domestic Marketing: Adheres to a single set of laws and regulations, making compliance more straightforward.

International Marketing: Requires compliance with multiple legal systems, including international trade laws, tariffs, and local regulations. This can complicate operations and increase the risk of legal issues.

5. Market Research and Analysis

Domestic Marketing: Market research is often more straightforward due to the familiarity with the local market and available data.

International Marketing: Requires extensive research to understand foreign markets. This includes studying local consumer preferences, competitive landscapes, and potential market entry barriers.

6. Distribution Channels

Domestic Marketing: Distribution channels are typically well-established and familiar.

International Marketing: Involves developing new distribution networks, which can be challenging due to logistical issues, different infrastructure, and the need to establish relationships with local partners.

7. Communication and Language

Domestic Marketing: Communication is generally in the marketer's native language, with a consistent message across the market.

International Marketing: Requires multilingual communication and adapting messages to resonate with different cultural contexts. This includes translating and localising content to avoid misunderstandings or offending local sensibilities.

8. Brand Positioning

Domestic Marketing: A single brand positioning strategy is usually sufficient.

International Marketing: May require different positioning strategies for different markets, considering local competition and consumer perceptions.

9. Risk and Uncertainty

Domestic Marketing: Generally involves lower risk due to familiarity with the market.

International Marketing: Entails higher risk due to political, economic, and social uncertainties in foreign markets. Companies must be prepared to handle unexpected changes and challenges.

10. Budgeting and Finances

Domestic Marketing: Budgeting is relatively straight forward with predictable costs.

International Marketing: Involves higher costs due to factors like international travel, translation services, tariffs, and currency exchange rates. Budgeting must account for these additional expenses and potential financial risks.

International and Global Marketing: A Distinction

Both International and Global Marketing are concerned with marketing across borders. Still, there exists a fundamental difference in their approach to market adaptation.

In International Marketing, the focus is on customising the entire marketing mix to suit the specific needs and preferences of each local market.

By implication this could mean:

- altering the product features
- adapting the advertising language and visuals

- changing the pricing strategy to match local economic conditions

The underlying aim of International Marketing is to resonate with the local consumer base while maintaining the core brand identity.

Global Marketing, on the other hand, adopts a "one-size-fits-all" approach. The same products and marketing strategies are applied uniformly across all markets with minimal intervention.

International vs Global Marketing: The Choice Criteria

Confronted with the choice of the better approach between International and Global Marketing, it all depends on the product, brand, and target markets.

International Marketing is better suited for products requiring adaptation or markets with strong cultural preferences.

Global Marketing is ideal for standardised products having universal appeal.

Wrapping Up

International marketing involves the strategic process of promoting and selling products or services across national borders. It requires a deep understanding of diverse cultural, economic, and legal environments too effectively meet the needs of global consumers.

PART 5
A RINGSIDE VIEW

"Don't bunt. Aim out of the ballpark. Aim for the company of immortals. International marketing requires boldness and creativity to truly stand out in a crowded global marketplace."

*- David Ogilvy, **Advertising Tycoon***

CHAPTER 6

VISTAS OF INTERNATIONAL MARKETING

Step into the world stage—international marketing made it easy for small businesses.

Strategic international marketing entails an in-depth analysis prior to entry into the potential market -so vital for SME businesses.

Parameters involving the action are:

Market Research and Analysis

- Market selection
- Competitor analysis
- Consumer behaviour

Cultural Appreciation

- Cultural sensitivity
- Localisation

Regulatory and Legal Considerations Compliance

- Trade Barriers

Entry Strategies

- Exporting

- Joint ventures
- Franchising
- Direct investment

Marketing and Promotion

- Digital marketing
- Local partnerships
- Trade shows and events

Pricing Strategy

- Cost analysis
- Competitive pricing

Distribution and Supply Chain Management

- Logistics .
- Local partnerships

Risk Management

- Financial risks
- Political risks
- Legal risks

Continuous Monitoring and Adaptation

- Market feedback
- Performance metrics

Guard against Common Mistakes

Navigating the multifaceted realm of international marketing can be akin to manoeuvring through a labyrinth of distinct customs, behaviours, and market dynamics. It is always advisable to guard against some Common Mistakes committed in the process:

- **Over-Reliance on Home Market Tactics:** It is never advisable to place over-reliance on marketing tactics applied in the home market.

- **Underestimating Regulatory Differences:** Overlooking subtle policy nuances can hinder campaign effectiveness leading to legal complications.

- **Neglecting Local Digital Ecosystems:** Besides Google and Facebook, avoiding use of local giants into digital strategies and ecosystems can lead to loss of substantial segments of the audience.

- **Overgeneralising Regions:** The cultural and economic landscape can vary dramatically even between neighbouring countries. Hence, treating Asia, Africa as monolithic entities will be a gross mistake.

- **Not Adapting to Local Payment Systems:** Ignoring consumer preferences for payment systems can hamper transaction completion rates e.g. credit cards versus mobile payment platforms or bank transfers.

- **Inconsistent Brand Messaging:** It is crucial to maintain consistent core brand values and messaging across markets in order to make the brand recognisable and resonating with local audiences.

- **Failure to Regularly Review and Iterate:** International market warrants regular review of strategies to remain competitive and relevant.

Challenges of International Marketing

International marketing poses numerous challenges that businesses must navigate to achieve success. These challenges can significantly impact marketing strategies and operations.

Cultural Differences

Cultural differences affect consumer behaviour, preferences, communication styles, and business practices. Cultural Differences primarily touch upon:

- **Consumer Behaviour:** Cultural norms and values influence purchasing decisions.
  For example, in some cultures, collectivism and family-orientation may drive buying behaviours.
  On the other hand, in other cases individualism may be more prominent.

- **Communication Styles:** Japan and China rely heavily on non-verbal cues and implicit messages. However, cultures such as the United States, Germany emphasise direct and explicit communication.

- **Business Etiquette:** Understanding local business customs and etiquette is essential for building relationships and negotiating deals. This includes knowing appropriate greetings, meeting protocols, and gift-giving practices.

- **Language Barriers:** Language barriers can hinder effective communication and marketing efforts.

Key issues related to language barriers, inter alia, include:

- **Translation and Localisation:** Marketing materials, product information, and customer support must be accurately translated. It should be localised to resonate with local audiences -adapting idiomatic expressions, cultural references, and humour.

- **Brand Messaging:** To ensure that brand messages are consistent and culturally appropriate across different languages is challenging because miscommunication can lead to misunderstanding. Eventually, it can damage brand reputation.

- **Customer Interaction:** Providing customer service and support in the local language is crucial for customer satisfaction and loyalty.

Key economic challenges

- **Purchasing Power:** Differences in income levels and purchasing power influence the product affordability and demand. It is, therefore, imperative that the pricing strategies are tailored to local economic conditions.

- **Economic Stability:** Economic instability, inflation, and currency fluctuations can disrupt marketing plans and affect profitability.

- **Market Development:** In emerging markets adapting to infrastructure, and market development levels is essential for effective distribution and logistics. As a result, it facilitates successful market entry and operations.

Strategies to Combat Challenges

The notable strategies to combat the challenges are:

Addressing Cultural Differences

- **Cultural Research:** Conduct comprehensive research on the cultural norms, values, and behaviours of the target market to tailor marketing strategies to local preferences.

- **Cultural Sensitivity Training:** Businesses must impart cultural sensitivity training for marketing teams and employees. It requires improved interactions with local stakeholders.

- **Local Partnerships:** Collaborate with local partners- distributors, agencies, and consultants - as they have in-depth knowledge of the local culture.

- **Adaptation and Customisation:** Adaptation and customisation of marketing messages, and campaigns to align with local cultural preferences helps to resonate better with local consumers.

Overcoming Language Barriers

- **Professional Translation Services:** It is advisable to use professional translation services to ensure accurate and culturally appropriate translation of marketing materials, product information, and customer support content.

- **Localisation Experts:** Engage localisation experts who understand the cultural context and nuances of the target language.

- **Multilingual Customer Support:** Train support staff to handle inquiries and interactions in the local language.

- **Consistent Brand Messaging:** For maintaining brand integrity and coherence, it is necessary to develop guidelines for brand messaging that ensure consistency across languages.

Navigating Economic Factors

- **Market Segmentation:** Segment markets based on economic conditions and purchasing power. Develop targeted strategies for different segments to optimise pricing and product offerings.

- **Flexible Pricing Strategies:** Implement flexible pricing strategies such as dynamic pricing or tiered pricing based on local economic conditions.

- **Risk Management:** Monitor economic indicators and implement risk management strategies to mitigate the impact of economic instability and currency fluctuations. It is convenient to take resort to hedging, diversifying investments, and maintaining financial reserves.

- **Infrastructure Adaptation:** Partnering with local logistics providers and investing in supply chain improvements greatly helps distribution and logistics strategies to suit local infrastructure conditions.

Wrapping Up

The scope of international marketing is vast, encompassing everything from product adaptation to global distribution channels. Its nature is dynamic, requiring businesses to be agile and responsive to the ever-changing global market conditions.

PART 6
GLOBAL MARKET ENVIRONMENT

"As we expand globally, it's crucial to remain agile and responsive to the needs of different markets. Our success depends on our ability to innovate and adapt quickly, while staying true to our core values and mission."

- Mary Barra, CEO of General Motors

CHAPTER 7
SCANNING THE ENVIRONMENT

Going global? Here's why small businesses are thriving in international markets.

While exploring potential for international marketing various aspects for the selected market would merit serious consideration:

- stage of economic development attained
- legal and regulatory systems
- factors that can impact ease of entry
- growth opportunities
- marketing strategies

Markets can be categorised as:

Developed Markets

Countries coming under the ambit of developed markets are characterised by:

- advanced economic structures
- high per capita income
- sophisticated business environments
- stable legal and regulatory frameworks

These developed markets are conducive to reliable and highly competitive space for international transactions.

Emerging Markets

Emerging markets are characterised as countries with rapidly growing economies offering significant growth opportunities. However, they come with attendant risks due to:

- political instability
- economic volatility
- less mature regulatory environments

Frontier Markets

Frontier markets suffer from unexplored potential for businesses.

The negative factors here are:

- under-developed infrastructure
- political instability
- nascent regulatory systems

Economic Environment

The economic environment encompasses the overall health of the economy in which businesses operate. The factors influencing consumer purchasing power, business investment and overall economic stability are reflected in key indicators:

- GDP growth rates
- inflation rates

- employment levels
- interest rates

Emerging markets often exhibit higher growth rates but come with increased risk.

The developed markets, on the other hand, tend to offer stability with slower growth.

Exchange rates also play a crucial role, impacting:

- cost of doing business internationally
- competitiveness of exports and imports

Political Environment

The political environment involves the stability and policies of governments in different countries.

Political stability is essential for a predictable business climate. Political instability can lead to risks such as expropriation, corruption, and policy changes.

Government policies on trade, tariffs, and foreign direct investment (FDI) significantly affect international business operations.

Political relations between countries can lead to trade agreements that facilitate business or conflicts that hinder it.

Legal Environment

The legal environment includes the framework of laws and regulations that govern business operations in various countries. This encompasses:

- intellectual property rights
- contract laws
- labor laws
- environmental regulations
- compliance with international laws, trade regulations
- and anti-corruption laws are critical for global businesses
- differences in legal systems-common law vs. civil law- can affect contract enforcement and dispute resolution

Cultural Environment

The cultural environment pertains to the values, beliefs, customs, and behaviours of different societies.

Understanding cultural differences is essential for effective marketing, management, and negotiations.

Elements such as language, religion, social norms, and business etiquette vary widely across regions and influence consumer preferences and employee interactions.

Cultural sensitivity and adaptability are crucial for building strong relationships and successful market entry.

Technological Environment

The technological environment encompasses the state of technological advancement and innovation in different regions. It includes :

- availability and adoption of digital technologies
- research and development (R&D) capabilities
- infrastructure such as telecommunications and transportation

Technological advancements can create new opportunities for:

- product development
- process improvements
- market expansion.

However, they also pose challenges such as cybersecurity threats. They warrant continuous innovation.

A strategic approach that considers these elements can help businesses mitigate risks and capitalise on global opportunities.

Wrapping Up

The global market environment is shaped by a complex mix of economic, political, technological, and cultural factors. Businesses must stay informed and adaptable to thrive amidst the uncertainties and opportunities presented by this dynamic landscape.

PART 7
CRAFTING AN INTERNATIONAL MARKETING STRATEGY

"The globalisation of markets is at hand. With that, the multinational commercial world nears its end, and so does the multinational marketer."

- Ted Levitt, Economist and Harvard Business School Professor

CHAPTER 8

ON TO STRATEGIC FRAMEWORK

The world is your market—start your small business's global journey today!

In an increasingly globalised world, the allure of international markets presents an unprecedented opportunity for businesses to expand their horizons and achieve significant growth.

Engaging in international marketing is vitally imperative for companies aspiring to become global leaders.

The dynamics of international marketing offer a myriad of benefits that can propel a business to:

- heights of success
- fostering innovation
- enhancing brand reputation
- driving sustainable profitability

As we delve into the strategic framework for crafting an effective international marketing strategy, it is essential to understand the profound advantages this approach brings to the table.

International marketing strategies are the backbone of a business's global expansion efforts providing:

- a roadmap for successful entry into new markets
- securing a competitive advantage

Strategic planning and execution help the businesses to:

- enhance their market share
- appeal to target customers in different cultures to achieve sustainable growth on a global scale.

Fundamental Principles of International Marketing

- Understanding customer behaviour through market analysis focusing on such factors as location, age, and purchasing behaviours.
- Tailoring the marketing message to the specific needs and preferences of international consumers in different countries–from packaging and pricing.
- Choosing the best international marketing sales channels through researching the cultural and social habits of the region and partnering with local people who can give you strategic insights.
- Creating a specific marketing budget with clearly defined timelines and built-in flexibility to adapt to a new customer base.
- Establishing a set of Key Performance Indicators (KPIs) which will give precise data for an accurate picture of your progress.

A Range of 10 Relevant Questions

While formulating international marketing strategy, it would be worthwhile exploring answers to 10 relevant questions.

It is pertinent to ponder over a set of questions before embarking on Strategic International Marketing.

1. Your aim to achieve.
2. Opting for creating a new market or entering an existing one.
3. Name of countries or regions supporting your business most.
4. Major demographics in your market.
5. Reasons why customers love your product.
6. Locations where the competitors are most active.
7. Competitive advantage enjoyed in potential markets.
8. Future potential to improve and scale up.
9. Nature of the peculiarities of your potential markets.
10. To opt for a single brand story or different messaging for different markets.

The answers to these questions will set you on the right path to creating a well-rounded international marketing strategy.

Role of Technology and Data- Driven Insights

A well-structured international marketing strategy involves:

- a comprehensive approach that utilises modern technologies
- data-driven insights to maximise effectiveness and efficiency

A list of actions involved in this context are:

Leverage Predictive Analytics to Forecast

Predictive Analytics is applied to gauge:

- market trends
- consumer behaviour
- potential future demands in different international markets
- areas and timing -when and where- marketing efforts should be concentrated to achieve maximum impact and improve ROI.

Collect, Assimilate and Utilise Account Insights

Utilise advanced data analytics tools to collect insights about target accounts in each international market covering:

- assessment of the business size, industry, market position
- specific needs of these accounts to tailor marketing strategies effectively

Implement Targeted Advertising

Ad targeting should consider segmentation of the market. It should focus on demographics that are responsive to the offerings.

Advertising should be adapted to local languages and cultural nuances to achieve relevance and effectiveness.

Personalise Content

To resonate with local tastes and expectations, customise content to serve the preferences and needs of different international audiences across all platforms and channels- from email marketing to social media and websites.

Continuously Monitor and Optimise Campaigns

Use performance metrics to refine strategies, improve personalisation, and increase the overall effectiveness of targeted advertising.

Stages of International Marketing Strategy

Essentially, formulation of International Marketing Strategy rests on 3 Stages:

- Analysis
- Choice
- Execution

Stage 1: Analysis

Covering the parameters such as:

Goal setting: Establish specific objectives and targets, ensuring alignment with the company's expansion goals.

Market research involving - Collection of data on:

- market size
- growth potential
- customer demographics
- trends

For each target market - understand the cultural nuances and legal requirements, including language, customs, regulations, and any potential barriers to entry.

Competitive analysis: Analyse competitors in the target market. Identify their strengths, weaknesses, market share, and strategies. This will help in positioning your company effectively.

SWOT analysis: Conduct a SWOT analysis to assess your company's internal capabilities and external factors that may impact your international expansion.

Market entry assessment: Evaluate various market entry options such as exporting, licensing, joint ventures, or establishing a wholly-owned subsidiary.

Stage 2: Choice

Encompasses the under-noted aspects:

Target market segmentation: Define your target audience within the international market based on demographics, psychographics, and behavioural factors.

Value proposition: Develop a unique value proposition tailored to each target market. Highlight how your product or service meets the specific needs and preferences of the target audience.

Positioning strategy: Create a market positioning strategy that:

- sets you apart from competitors
- determines how you want your brand to be perceived

Pricing strategy: Establish a pricing strategy that factors in:

- local market conditions
- competitive pricing
- cost consideration aligning with your value proposition

Distribution and Promotion Channels: Ensure careful selection of channels for promotion of your product so that it can efficiently reach the target audience.

This may involve partnerships with local distributors or the E-commerce platforms.

Stage 3: Execution

The factors to be considered are:

- **Localisation:** Tailor your product, marketing materials, and communication to align seamlessly with the local culture and language.

- **Marketing and Promotion:** Execute marketing campaigns tailored to the international market. This may involve digital marketing, advertising, social media, and other relevant channels.

- **Sales:** Ensure your product is readily available to customers through your chosen channels of distribution.

- **Monitoring:** Continuously monitor the performance of your international marketing efforts. Gather feedback, track key performance indicators (KPIs), and be prepared to tweak the required adjustments.

- **Compliance and Risk management:** Ensure full compliance with local laws and regulations.

Develop a risk management plan to address potential challenges such as currency fluctuations, political instability, or supply chain disruptions.

Creation of A Strategic Roadmap

Connotation of International Marketing Strategy:

International Marketing Strategy refers to a plan that businesses use to:

- identify their target markets
- understand their needs
- create a marketing plan
- attract and engage those target markets

There are three main components to any successful international marketing strategy:

- Market research
- Product development
- Distribution

Market research helps businesses understand their target markets. Businesses need to know:

- what products to produce
- how to price them
- how to distribute them
- who their target market is
- what the target market wants

Product development determines

- which products to produce
- how to produce them
- what features to include in their products
- how much to charge for them

- where to sell them
- which markets to focus on

Distribution determines

- how to get products into the hands of the target market
- where to produce their products
- how much to charge for them
- how to market them
- who will distribute their products

Target Market Selection

A number of factors are considered when selecting a target market:

- type and nature of product or service
- country or region in which the target market resides
- economic conditions of that country or region

Competitive Analysis

Competitive analysis can be broken down into five key steps:

- **Understanding the Competition**
  To understand the competition by reading industry reports, interviewing industry experts, or conducting online surveys.

- **Understanding the Market**
  Involves understanding the:
  - demographics of the target market
  - buying habits of the target market
  - competition in the market
- **Understanding the Customer**
  Involves understanding what customers want and how they want it delivered.
- **Understanding the Business**
  Involves understanding the company's strengths and weaknesses, as well as its competitive environment.
- **Creating a Strategy**
  Involves developing a plan that will guide your efforts in beating the competition.

Positioning and Differentiation

Five main positioning strategies are:

- **Positioning as the best in class:** Entails positioning your business as the best in its field. You are required to identify your target market's needs and offer them a product or service that is better than what they can find elsewhere.

- **Positioning as unique:** Need to identify your target market's needs and offer them a product or service that is not available from any other source.

- **Positioning as affordable:** Need to identify your target market's needs and offer them a product or service that is affordable compared to what they can find elsewhere.

- **Positioning as convenient:** Required to identify your target market's needs and offer them a product or service that is convenient for them.

- **Positioning as aspirational:** Required to identify your target market's needs and offer them something that makes them feel like they could be successful if they chose to pursue it.

Product Strategy

There are a number of different factors to consider when choosing a product for the international market.

Cultural Differences: When designing a product for the international market, the cultural differences between countries must be taken into account. The design of a product must appeal to all cultures, and not just one.

Consumer Preferences: The company must design products to satisfy the preferences of consumers.

Economic Indicators: A detailed research of economic indicators enables decisions about the products.

Pricing Strategy

It is essential to price the product to make it profitable, while still meeting customer needs.

Factors to consider when pricing a product for the international include:

- local economic indicators, cultural preferences, and customer needs
- sustainable pricing

Sustainability refers to pricing a product to avoid any negative consequences on the environment or consumers in the long-term.

Promotion Strategy

Promotion can be divided into two categories:

- direct marketing
- indirect marketing

Direct marketing refers to marketing campaigns that are aimed directly at consumers.

Indirect marketing refers to marketing campaigns that are not aimed directly at consumers.

The choice of strategy is dictated by increased sales at minimised costs.

Distribution and Logistics

International marketing is the process of designing, executing, and measuring the effectiveness of marketing programs in international markets.

Distribution refers to the channels through which products or services are delivered to customers. The distribution channel can be physical or digital.

Logistics refers to the activities involved in moving products from the producer to the consumer.

Physical distribution channels include distribution through a retailer.

Digital distribution channels include delivery through the internet. The logistics channel is important for international marketing because it determines how quickly products or services can be delivered to customers.

The logistics channel can be physical or digital.

Physical logistics channels include manufacturing, warehousing, shipping, and delivery.

Manufacturing is the process of creating a product.

Warehousing is the storage facility where products are kept before they are delivered to the customer.

Shipping is the transportation of products from one location to another.

Delivery is the process of delivering products to the customer.

Distribution refers to the channels through which products or services are delivered to customers.

Monitoring and Evaluation

Monitoring and evaluation help to ensure that an international marketing strategy is achieving its desired results.

Evaluation can be used to:

- identify the overall effectiveness of the strategy
- identify areas in which the strategy could be improved
- determine whether the costs associated with the strategy are justified

Some of the most common methods to measure the effectiveness of an international marketing strategy are:

- **Surveys** are useful because they allow marketers to measure how people are using the product or service and how they feel about it. Focus groups can be used to generate insights about how people think about the product or service and how they would like it to be improved.

- **Audits** can be used to examine how well the organisation is implementing the international marketing strategy.

- **Evaluation** can also be used to identify areas in which the strategy could be improved.Finally, evaluation can help determine whether the costs associated with the strategy are justified.

Risk Management

The process of Risk Management helps organisations to identify, assess, and reduce the risks associated with their business operations.

Risk management can be used to improve the efficiency and effectiveness of an organisation's decision-making processes, and to protect its assets.

There are five main types of risks that organisations face:

1. **Financial risks** include risks associated with investments, loans, and credit ratings. Financial risks can be reduced by using sound financial planning practices and by monitoring financial reports regularly.

2. **Environmental risks** include risks associated with chemical spills, natural disasters, and terrorist attacks. Environmental risks can be reduced by using safety procedures and by monitoring environmental reports regularly.

3. **Legal risks** include risks associated with antitrust action, copyright infringement, and patent litigation. Legal risks can be reduced by using due diligence procedures and by monitoring legal reports regularly.

4. **Technical risks** include risks associated with computer viruses, hacking attacks, and defective products. Technical risks can be reduced by implementing security measures and by monitoring technical reports regularly.

5. **Social risks** include risks associated with customer dissatisfaction, public opinion, and employee turnover. Social risks can be reduced by developing customer service policies and by monitoring social media reports regularly.

Significance of Automation

Leveraging Automation tools can yield the following **Advantages:**

- **Improved consistency and accuracy:** Automation tools can reduce errors and inconsistencies in marketing materials across different markets.

- **Time and cost savings:** Automating repetitive tasks, such as social media scheduling, content publishing, or email marketing, can save businesses valuable time and resources.

Two concepts of relevance which have assumed importance in international marketing are:

Cultural Sensitivity

Cultural sensitivity in international marketing refers to the awareness and consideration of the cultural differences and nuances that exist among different markets.

Cultural Sensitivity underscores respecting the customs, values, traditions, and social norms off the target audience to create marketing strategies that resonate and avoid cultural missteps.

Role of Cultural Sensitivity

- **Building Trust and Relationships:** Cultural sensitivity helps in building trust and fostering long-term relationships with customers. It demonstrates respect and understanding which can lead to greater brand loyalty.

- **Avoiding Offence:** Misunderstanding cultural differences can lead to offensive marketing, damaging a brand's reputation. Culturally insensitive campaigns can result in backlash, boycotts, and loss of market share.

- **Enhanced Communication:** Cultural sensitivity ensures that the message is conveyed in a manner that is relatable and acceptable to the target audience.

Strategies for Implementing Cultural Sensitivity

- **Cultural Research:** Conduct thorough research to understand language, religion, social norms, and consumer behaviour of the target market.

- **Diverse Teams:** Diverse teams can help in crafting culturally sensitive marketing strategies.

- **Localised Content:** Adapt marketing content to reflect the cultural preferences of the target audience. This may include using local languages, symbols, and references that are familiar and appealing.

- **Feedback Mechanisms:** Engage with local stakeholders and customers to gain insights and improve cultural sensitivity.

Localisation

Localisation in international marketing refers to the process of adapting products, services, and marketing content to meet the specific needs and preferences of a particular market.

Localisation involves modifying elements such as language, design, packaging, and promotional strategies to align with local tastes and cultural norms.

Role of Localisation

- **Relevance:** Localisation makes a brand's offerings more relevant to local consumers, increasing the likelihood of acceptance and success in the market.

- **Competitive Advantage:** Localised strategies can provide a competitive edge by differentiating a brand from competitors who may adopt a one-size-fits-all approach.

- **Increased Engagement:** Tailoring marketing efforts to local preferences enhances customer engagement and drives better results.

Strategies for Effective Localisation

- **Language Adaptation:** Translate and adapt marketing content to the local language, ensuring accuracy and cultural appropriateness. This includes literal translation, idioms, slang, and right context.

- **Cultural Alignment:** Modify visuals, symbols, colour, meanings, imagery and cultural references themes to align with local cultural preferences.
- **Local Partnerships:** Collaborate with local influencers, businesses, and organisations to build credibility and trust within the community.
- **Product Modification:** Adjust product features, packaging, pricing, flavours and sizes to suit local tastes and purchasing power.

Wrapping Up

The parameters of international marketing include understanding market entry strategies, pricing models, cultural sensitivities, and legal regulations.

These factors are crucial for developing effective marketing campaigns that resonate with international audiences.

PART 8
A STRATEGIC FUSION

"Globalisation has made the world more interconnected than ever. The next frontier in international marketing will be mastering the art of local relevance while leveraging global scale."

- John Quelch (Professor of Business Administration at Harvard Business School)

CHAPTER 9
STRATEGIES GALORE

Turn your small business into a global brand with these international marketing secrets.

In today's globalised economy, the opportunity for small businesses to expand their reach beyond domestic borders is more achievable than ever. However, entering the international market is not merely about replicating what works locally. Rather, it requires a strategic approach that accounts for diverse cultures, regulations, and market dynamics.

Now join me in a journey of Fusion of Marketing Strategies for **Marketing Beyond Borders**. These Strategies are designed specifically for small businesses looking to compete on a global stage.

By mastering these strategies, you can unlock new growth opportunities, build a resilient brand presence across borders, and drive your business to unprecedented heights.

The Curtain Raiser

Today, we unlock the doors to international marketing—where the vastness of the world narrows into a realm of endless potential. As the curtain rises, imagine your brand. It is not confined to familiar territories.

It has turned into a force ready to navigate and conquer diverse markets across the globe.

Here, we'll unravel strategies that transform every challenge into an opportunity and every market into a potential ally.

The strategies that transform challenges into triumphs, and competition into collaboration will ignite your global vision and imagination.

We devise the art and science of reaching across oceans and continents.

We will be creating connections that resonate on a world stage. In a way, we shall launch your brand's global odyssey.

You will positively witness here an Amalgam of International Marketing Strategies, good enough to Market Beyond Borders.

Venturing into international markets can seem daunting, Nevertheless, with a well-crafted strategic approach, even small businesses can thrive on a global scale.

The insights shared in this chapter are about:

- reaching new customers
- understanding them
- adapting to their unique needs
- positioning your business as a trusted and valuable player in the global marketplace.

As you implement these strategies, remember that success in international marketing is not about size, but about being smart, agile, and committed to continuous learning and adaptation.

With the right strategy, your small business can achieve big results on the international stage.

STRATEGY 1
MARKET RESEARCH AND ANALYSIS

The Art of Identifying Lucrative Markets in International Business.

International Market Research helps small businesses in a new market to understand the needs, preferences, and behaviour of the potential customers.

Connotation of Market Research

International market research is the process of collecting and analysing data from different countries and regions to identify the best opportunities and strategies for your business.

Market Research and Analysis

Market research is the systematic collection and analysis of information about the marketplace or consumer behaviour in order to develop effective marketing strategies. It encompasses a wide range of activities from surveying customers to conducting focus groups.

The goal of market research is to improve the effectiveness of a company's marketing efforts by understanding customer needs and wants.

Market research can help identify potential product or service deficiencies and suggest ways to fix them.

By understanding the competition, market researchers can develop strategies to stay ahead of the curve.

Utility of Market Research

Market Research can help in identifying :

- target customers and their characteristics
- current trends
- demands in the market
- cultural, social, and legal factors
- competitors and their strengths and weaknesses
- differentiating methods of product or service

Three main types of market research are:

- Qualitative
- Quantitative
- Mixed

Qualitative market research: is based on personal observation and interviews with consumers.

It is used to:

- develop ideas for new products or services
- understand customer needs and desires
- evaluate customer satisfaction

Quantitative market research

- uses statistical methods to measure consumer behaviour
- helps companies determine which products or services are selling well
- how to improve marketing campaigns

Mixed market research

Mixed market research combines both qualitative and quantitative techniques.

Mixed market research is:

- used to understand customer needs in combination with sales data
- used to evaluate customer satisfaction
- used to determine which channels are most effective for reaching customers

Conducting International Marketing Research: Major Steps

1. Define research objectives and scope.
2. Select research methods and sources.
3. Data analysis and interpretation.
4. Apply the results to your marketing strategy.

Based on your research findings, it is possible to develop the marketing strategy for each market considering the following aspects:

- Market segmentation
- Targeting
- Positioning
- Marketing- mix

Effective market research is the cornerstone of successful international marketing. It provides the insights needed to understand:

- target markets
- evaluate potential opportunities
- make informed strategic decisions

International market research entails a mix of traditional and modern methods and tools.

Sources of Market Research are:

- **Primary Research**

Surveys and Questionnaires: Surveys can be conducted online, via email, or through face-to-face interviews. Questionnaires should be designed to capture specific information about consumer preferences, purchasing behaviour, and product perceptions.

Focus Groups: Focus groups involve guided discussions with a small group of target consumers. This method provides deeper insights into consumer attitudes, motivations, and cultural nuances. It is useful for exploring new markets and testing marketing concepts.

In-Depth Interviews: One-on-one interviews with industry experts, customers, or business partners can yield valuable qualitative data..

Observational Research: Observing consumer behaviour in natural settings can provide insights that are not easily captured through direct questioning. This method helps understand how consumers interact with products and make purchasing decisions.

- **Secondary Research**

Industry Reports: These are invaluable for gaining a macro-level understanding of international markets.

Academic Journals and Publications: Research papers and articles from academic journals offer theoretical insights and empirical data on consumer behaviour, marketing strategies, and international business practices. Online Databases are essential for obtaining up-to-date and reliable data.

Competitor Websites and Financial Reports: This information helps identify market gaps and opportunities for differentiation.

- **Analysing Target Demographics**

Cultural Analysis: Cultural analysis helps identify the preferences and behaviours that influence consumer decisions in different regions.

Economic Analysis: Assessing the economic environment provides insights into the purchasing power and potential demand for products and services.

Technological Analysis: Evaluating the level of technological adoption and internet penetration helps determine the most effective marketing channels and strategies for reaching target audiences.

- **Competitor Analysis**

Competitor analysis is a critical component of market research. It involves identifying and evaluating the strengths and weaknesses of existing and potential competitors to inform strategic decision-making.

Identifying Competitors

Direct Competitors: Identifying direct competitors helps understand the competitive landscape and benchmark performance.

Indirect Competitors: Analysing indirect competitors provides insights into alternative solutions available to consumers.

Potential Competitors: Monitoring potential competitors helps anticipate market changes and prepare proactive strategies.

Evaluating Competitors

SWOT Analysis: Conducting a SWOT analysis -Strengths, Weaknesses, Opportunities, Threats- for each competitor provides a comprehensive overview of their market position. SWOT analysis helps identify areas where your business can compete effectively and capitalise on competitor weaknesses.

Product Analysis: Product analysis of products of competitors includes evaluating the product lifecycle and innovation strategies.

Marketing Strategy Analysis: Analysing competitors' marketing strategies, including their messaging, advertising channels, promotions, and customer engagement tactics, provides insights into effective marketing practices and areas for improvement.

Financial Performance Analysis: Financial analysis includes examining funding sources and investment strategies.

Customer Feedback and Reviews: Analysing customer feedback and online reviews of competitors' products and services provides valuable insights into consumer satisfaction and areas where competitors may be falling short.

Wrapping Up

Market research and analysis emphasises the importance of thorough understanding of the target audience and market conditions. Accurate data collection and interpretation drive informed decision-making, helping businesses stay competitive and identify opportunities. Ultimately, effective research and analysis serves as the foundation for successful marketing strategies and business growth.

STRATEGY 2
BUDGETING, FINANCIAL PLANNING AND RISK MANAGEMENT

Stretch Every Rupee: Master the Art of Budgeting to Fuel Your International Expansion.

For small businesses venturing into international markets, budgeting and financial planning are critical to ensuring sustainable growth and success. Strategic international marketing essentially necessitates meticulous actions in the following areas:

- Budgeting
- Financial Planning
- Allocation Strategy
- Cost Estimation

- Risk Management

Role of Budgeting in Strategic International Marketing

Resource Allocation: Effective budgeting ensures that resources are allocated efficiently across various marketing activities such as :

- market research
- advertising
- localisation
- distribution

Cost Control: Budgeting helps in monitoring and controlling costs. It is essential for maintaining profitability while exploring new markets with different cost structures.

Risk Management: Entering international markets involves various risks including :

- currency fluctuations
- political instability
- regulatory changes

Budgeting allows for the creation of contingency funds to manage these risks.

Performance Measurement: Budgets set financial benchmarks that help in measuring the performance of international marketing campaigns, enabling small businesses to assess their return on investment (ROI).

Principal Expenditure Heads

- Market research and entry costs
- Localisation and cultural adaptation
- Regulatory compliance
- Marketing and promotion
- Logistics and distribution

Financial Planning

1. Cash Flow Management

Ensuring a steady cash flow to support ongoing marketing activities and operational expenses in international markets is very essential.

Planning for longer payment cycles that might be prevalent in certain international markets is required.

2. Investment in Technology

Investing in technology and CRM systems to manage international customer relationships and streamline marketing efforts is quite essential.

This is equally important for Budgeting for e-commerce platforms, online payment systems, and digital marketing tools to reach global audiences.

3. Scenario Planning

Scenario Planning entails developing financial scenarios to anticipate different market conditions and their potential impact on the business.

It also involves creating flexible budgets that can be adjusted based on market responses and emerging opportunities or challenges.

4. Financial Risk Mitigation

Using hedging strategies to manage currency exchange risks and setting aside emergency funds to handle unexpected financial challenges in international markets are required for mitigating financial risk.

Budgeting & Decision-Making Process

- Involves budgeting and financial planning that provides the data and insights needed to make informed decisions about market entry, expansion, and marketing strategies.
- Helps in prioritising markets and marketing activities based on financial feasibility and potential ROI.

Long-Term Sustainability

- Ensures that international marketing efforts are sustainable in the long run by balancing short-term gains with long-term financial health.

- Encourages disciplined financial management, reducing the risk of over extending resources.

Competitive Advantage

- Provides a competitive edge by enabling small businesses to allocate resources more effectively than competitors.
- Facilitates strategic investments in innovation, technology, and customer engagement that can differentiate the business in international markets.

Allocation Strategy

In the realm of international marketing, the allocation and management of financial resources play a crucial role in the success of any business venture.

Understanding the Significance of Budget Allocation

Appropriate allocation of financial resources enables businesses to ensure that their marketing campaigns:

- reach the right target audience
- maximise brand exposure
- generate desired outcomes

Efficient resource utilisation minimises the risk of overspending or underspending in different markets.

Factors Influencing Budget Allocation

When determining the allocation of financial resources for international marketing, several factors which exert influence are:

- market size
- competition
- consumer behaviour
- cultural nuances
- regulatory frameworks

Businesses can ensure optimal utilisation of resources by tailoring their budget allocation to specific markets.

Cruciality of Market Research

Market research aids effective budget allocation in international marketing. Businesses can :

- gain important insights into data- driven decisions when allocating financial resources.
- ensure that their marketing efforts align with market demands and yield favourable results.

Budgeting for International Marketing: Notable Steps

Assessing Costs

Identify and estimate the costs associated with international marketing activities.

Key cost categories include:
- Market research
- Market entry
- Marketing and promotion
- Localisation
- Logistics and distribution
- Personnel
- Technology

Allocating Resources

Allocation of resources is based on priorities and expected returns:

Prioritise High-Impact Activities: Focus on activities that are likely to generate the highest return on investment (ROI).

Balance Short-Term and Long-Term Goals: Ensure that the budget supports both:
- immediate objectives, such as market entry
- long-term goals, such as brand building and customer retention

Flexibility: Provide for flexibility in the budget to accommodate unexpected opportunities.

Set aside a contingency fund to manage unforeseen expenses.

Monitoring and Adjusting

Regularly monitor spending against the budget and adjust as necessary. If certain strategies are not delivering the expected results, reallocate resources to more promising areas.

Risk Management Strategies

The key risks and strategies to manage them in international marketing are :

Market Risks

- **Economic Fluctuations:** Diversify market portfolio by entering multiple markets with different economic conditions.
- **Political Instability:** Stay informed about the political landscape. Develop contingency plans to respond to potential disruptions.

Competitive Risks

- **Intense Competition:** Conduct thorough competitor analysis to identify strengths and weaknesses. Differentiate your offerings by focusing on unique value propositions and leveraging your brand's strengths.

- **Market Saturation:** Consider niche markets segments where competition is less intense and your products can stand out.

Operational Risks

- **Supply Chain Disruptions:** Develop a resilient supply chain by diversifying suppliers, building buffer stocks, and implementing robust logistics management systems.
- **Regulatory Compliance:** Ensure compliance with local laws and regulations by working with legal experts and staying updated on changes in the regulatory landscape.

Financial Risks

- **Currency Fluctuations:** Use hedging strategies and financial instruments to manage currency risk. Further, price your products in local currencies to mitigate the impact of exchange rate fluctuations on customers.
- **Credit Risk:** Conduct thorough due diligence on potential partners and customers. Consider using credit insurance and secure payment terms to minimise the risk of non-payment.

Wrapping Up

Effective budgeting, financial planning, and risk management ensure that resources are allocated optimally to meet business goals while mitigating potential risks. By carefully forecasting and monitoring financial performance, businesses can navigate uncertainties, safeguard assets, and achieve long-term sustainability. Strategic financial management is key to balancing growth aspirations with financial stability.

STRATEGY3
MARKETING- MIX STRATEGY

Diverse Markets, One Strategy: Tailoring Your Marketing Mix for Global Success.

"One of the ways to make sure you have a thriving practice is always market. The best way to do is to systematise your marketing mix, so it runs on auto-pilot."

- Lisa A Mininni

The 4 Ps of Marketing Mix – Product, Place, Price and Promotion constitute the core principles to build a Marketing Strategy.

They direct the focus of the marketers to the area of right priorities.

These 4 Ps eventually enlarged their scope to 7 Ps bringing yet another dimension to the realm of marketing.

The marketers are able to take these vital actions by tailoring their Marketing - Mix Strategy:

- Adapt their Product, Price, Place, and Promotion Strategies for each target market.
- Modify the offerings by introducing the essential changes in features and packaging to meet local needs and regulations.
- Set prices by aligning with local purchasing power, buying behaviour, and competitor landscape.
- Develop culturally relevant marketing materials and messaging for each audience through localisation.

Framework of 7 Ps of Marketing -Mix consist of the actions brands take to market their products and services. They apply a framework of 7 core components:

Product, Place, Price ,Promotion, People, Process and Physical Evidence

Product

Product denotes the item or service that a company offers to its customers.

Product includes:

- physical product
- packaging
- branding

- design
- quality
- features
- benefits

The underlying goal is to create a product that caters to the needs and wants off the target market. The unique value sets it apart from competitors.

Place

Place refers to the location where customers can purchase the product or service and access it.

Place covers:

- distribution channels
- logistics
- market coverage
- levels of service

The underlying motto is to make the product easily accessible and available at the right time and place, for the right people.

Further, the businesses have to ensure that the product is available when and where customers need it through:

- inventory management
- order fulfilment
- shipping options

Price

Price component indicates the amount that customers pay for the product or service.

Price covers:
- cost of goods
- profit margins
- pricing strategy
- discounts
- promotional offers

The marketing strategy should set a price that is competitive.

It should necessarily reflect the value of the product aligning with profit goals of the business.

Pricing Strategy can, inter alia, be two-fold:

(a) Skimming Pricing Strategy sets a high price to appeal to customers who are willing to pay a premium for a unique product or experience.

(b) Penetration Pricing Strategy sets a low price to gain market share and attract price-sensitive customers.

Promotion

Promotion refers to various marketing tactics that a company uses to promote its products or services.

Promotion covers:

- Advertising
- Sales promotions
- Public relations
- Personal selling
- Digital marketing

The underlying objective of Promotion is to create awareness and interest in the product and persuade customers to make a purchase.

People

People element covers a category of individuals who are involved in the production, distribution, and consumption of the product or service.

People includes:

- employees
- customers
- suppliers
- partners

Process

Process implies how a business designs, creates, and delivers its products and services to its customers.

Physical Evidence

Physical Evidence refers to the tangible parts of products or services that can be delivered into the hands of customers.

Physical Evidence includes:

- a physical product, like a car, or
- a digital product, such as software.

The Physical Evidence provides proof of delivery to the customer.

Partners

P stands for Partners. It allows one to -identify and establish partnerships that can:

- help expand the reach
- improve customer service
- increase overall revenue of the business

Payment

Payment refers to the ways in which the businesses hold and process transactions and payments such as cash, credit cards, or online payment platforms.

Packaging

Packaging refers to the physical appearance and presentation of a company's products or services.

Perception

Perception can help the business to identify how its brand is perceived. The business can make changes to improve its overall image and customer experience.

Significance of 7Ps of Marketing - Mix

- Sets objectives and provides a roadmap for the business.
- Enables SWOT analysis.
- Facilitates review and definition of key issues of marketing of products or services.
- Enables evaluation of existing business.
- Facilitates marketing the right product to the right people at the right price and time.

Role of 4 Cs

In the 1990s, the 4 Cs were adopted to shift focus more from Business to Customer.

The 4 Cs are:

1. **Consumer:** The business has to keep focus on solving problems of consumers rather than creating products.
2. **Cost:** Cost includes the time taken to research a product and make a purchase.
3. **Convenience:** Convenience implies how easy or difficult it is for consumers to find and purchase a product.

4. **Communication:** Communication involves a dialogue between consumer and the seller.

Integration of 10 Pillars of International Marketing with Marketing - Mix

1. **People -** Understanding customer behaviour in a different world.

2. **Product -** Altering to fit the needs of the new market. In case the current offering of the product in the new market does not suit then there are two options:

   - decide not to sell in that market or
   - alter the offering to meet the local demand

3. **Price -** Choosing a premium or economy pricing strategy.

4. **Promotion -** Choosing strategies that work in a new environment.

5. **Place -** Finding the sales avenue that consumers use.

6. **Packaging -** Finding the right look and visual appearance.

7. **Positioning -** Determining which messages will resonate with the market the first time. The messaging should be derived from the **unique value proposition (UVP)**, which should be made up of the following:

   - **Relevancy** — how the product solves customers' problems or improves their lives.
   - **Value** — what are the specific benefits.

- **Differentiation** — why the ideal customers should choose your product over the competition.

8. **Physical Evidence** - Getting the ambiance and mood right. The physical evidence can be broken into three separate areas.

    - **Physical Environment:** The physical environment is the physical space that surrounds the consumer during the service. For selling food, the restaurant is a physical environment.

    - **Ambiance:** It is about the mood and feeling inside the physical space. Colours, music, and lighting can make a big difference when it comes to how your service is perceived by your consumers.

    - **Spatial Layout:** It is the significance of the actual layout of the space where your service is offered.

9. **Local Teams** - Don't overlook them, leverage your existing relationships, and make sure to give their feedback extra weight.

10. **Understanding** - making a positive influence on your new community.

11. **Brands that utilise the triple bottom line** — people, planet, and profit — tend to have more success as a global company.

Wrapping Up

The marketing mix, is the cornerstone of any successful marketing strategy. Each element must be carefully tailored to meet customer needs and market conditions, ensuring a cohesive approach that maximises impact. A well-balanced marketing mix drives brand value and aligns with the overall business objectives.

STRATEGY 4
GLOBAL MARKET SEGMENTATION

Unlock Global Potential: How Strategic Market Segmentation Can Transform Your Business.

"Market Segmentation is sub-dividing a market into distinct and homogeneous subgroups of customers, where any group can conceivably be selected as a target market to be met with distinct marketing mix"

- Philip Kotler

Market Segmentation is the process of dividing the target market into defined groups with specific characteristics.

It is a strategy of divide and conquer.

It divides the market to conquer it.

The purpose of segmentation is to identify distinct groups within the target market. It is then possible to deliver more targeted and niche-focused messaging and products.

Global market segmentation can be categorised into four types:

1. Behavioural Segmentation

Behavioural market segmentation categories the market based on their previous behaviour with your brand.

Some of the traits within this type include:

- purchase patterns
- previous purchases
- awareness of your business
- product rating

2. Demographic Segmentation

Demographic market segmentation focuses on who the customer is.

The traits placed in this segment depend on whether your business. is on a B2B or B2C basis.

Traits in B2B companies would include: industry type, company size, years of practice, and revenue range.

Traits in B2C companies would include age, education, gender, occupation, family status, and income.

3. Geographic Segmentation

Geographic market segmentation allows the business to split the market audience based on their location, which is a helpful purchase decision-making factor.

4. Psychographic Segmentation

Psychographic market segmentation separates markets based on their personalities.

Traits within this segmentation include: attitudes, values, and interests.

Wrapping Up

Global market segmentation allows businesses to identify and target specific customer groups across diverse markets. By tailoring strategies to meet the unique needs of each segment, companies can enhance relevance and build stronger connections with international audiences. Effective segmentation is crucial for optimising marketing efforts and achieving global reach.

STRATEGY 5 INTERNATIONAL MARKET ENTRY

Break Into New Markets: Proven Strategies for a Successful International Market Entry.

Market Entry Strategies serve businesses with a roadmap for entry into the realm of international markets.

The ultimate selection of Entry Mode is based on the goals and target of the market.

Market Entry Strategies: Connotation

Market entry strategies are methods companies use to plan, distribute and deliver goods to international markets.

The cost and level of a company's control over distribution can vary depending on the strategy it chooses.

Companies usually choose a strategy based on various considerations such as:

- type of product they sell
- value of the product
- whether shipping requires special handling procedures
- current competition and consumer needs

For selection of effective strategy, it is essential for the companies to align their budgets with their product considerations.

Selection Criteria

The three primary factors that affect a company's choice of international market entry strategy are:

Marketing to consider:

- which countries have their target market
- how they would market their product to this segment.

Sourcing to choose whether to :

- produce the products
- buy them
- work with a manufacturer overseas

Control to decide whether to:

- enter the market independently or
- partner with other businesses when presenting their products to international markets.

Utility of Market Entry Strategies

Market entry strategies play very useful role because:

- selling a product in an international market calls for precise planning and maintenance processes.

- helping companies to stay organised before, during and after entering new markets.

Creation of Market Entry Strategy

It is quite essential to consider specific regulations, competition, and market dynamics to develop a plan for entering new international markets. It involves:

Evaluating various market entry modes such as:

- exporting
- licensing
- joint ventures
- wholly-owned subsidiaries

Such evaluation is governed by:

- business objectives
- resources
- risk tolerance

Identifying key players, their strengths, weaknesses, and market positioning.

Assessing potential barriers to entry, such as tariffs, trade agreements, distribution challenges, or cultural differences.

Market Entry Strategies for International Markets

Each of the Market Entry Strategies for International Marketing reflect upon:

- concept
- mode of operation
- evaluation

Exporting

Exporting involves marketing the products in the countries of selected target markets.

There are two variations of exporting:

Direct exporting in which the exporters sell the product in international markets directly or without third-party involvement.
Companies that sell luxury products or have sold their goods in global markets in the past prefer to choose this method.

Indirect exporting is done by engaging the services of agents or international distributors.
Indirect exporting results in a higher return on investment (ROI) because the agents know the methods to succeed in the markets in which they work.

Piggybacking

Piggybacking strategy for market entry involves asking other businesses whether they can add your product to their overseas inventory.

In case your company and an international company agree to this arrangement, the implications are:

- both parties share the profit for each sale.

- your company can manage the risk of selling overseas by allowing its partner to handle international marketing while your company focuses on domestic retail.

Counter trade

Counter trade is a common form of indirect international marketing.
Counter trading functions as a barter system.

The companies trade each other's goods instead of offering their products for purchase.

The system does not have specific legal regulations. This means companies may solve problems like ensuring other companies understand the value of their products and attempting to acquire goods at a similar level of quality.

Counter trading is a cost-effective choice for many businesses because the practice may exempt them from import quotas.

Licensing

Under Licensing , one company transfers the right to use or sell a product to another company.

A company may choose this method if:

- it has a product that's in demand

- the company to which it plans to license should have a large market.

Joint Ventures

Joint ventures are created as an attempt to minimise the risk of entering an international market.

Joint ventures have the potential to earn more revenue than individual companies because they function like large independent companies rather than two smaller companies.

This market entry strategy carries the risk of an imbalance in company involvement.

Company Ownership

If your company plans to sell a product internationally without managing the shipment and distribution of the goods you produce, you might consider purchasing an existing company in the country in which you want to do business.

The strategy gives your organisation credibility as a local business which can help boost sales.

Company ownership costs more than most market entry strategies. However, it has the potential to lead to a high ROI.

Franchising

A franchise is a chain retail company in which an individual or group buyer pays for the right to manage company branches on the company's behalf.

Franchises exist globally They offer businesses the opportunity to expand overseas.

Franchising typically requires strong brand recognition, because consumers in the target market should know what you offer and have a desire to purchase it.

Franchising offers companies, with well-known brands , a way to earn a profit while taking an indirect management approach.

Outsourcing

Outsourcing involves hiring another company to manage certain aspects of business operations for your company.

It is concerned with making an agreement with another company to handle international product sales on your company's behalf.

Companies that choose to outsource may relinquish a certain amount of control over the sale of their products. However, they may justify this risk with the revenue they save on employment costs.

Greenfield Investments

Greenfield investments involve buying the land and resources to build a facility internationally. The staff is hired to run it.

Greenfield investments may subject a company to high risks and entail significant costs for the companies.

The advantage here is that they can help companies comply with government regulations in a new market.

These investments typically benefit large, established organisations as opposed to new enterprises.

Turnkey Projects

The term "turnkey" refers to the idea that the client can simply turn a key in a lock and enter a fully operational facility.

Turnkey projects apply specifically to companies that plan, develop and construct new buildings for their clients.

This market entry strategy is suitable if your clients comprise foreign government agencies.

Wrapping up

Entering international markets requires careful planning and strategy selection to overcome cultural, legal, and economic barriers. Choosing the right market entry mode—whether exporting, joint ventures, or direct investment—depends on market conditions and company objectives. Successful entry into new markets can unlock significant growth opportunities and expand global presence.

STRATEGY 6
PRODUCT ADAPTATION AND DEVELOPMENT

Adapt to Succeed: How Tailoring Your Product for Global Markets Can Unlock Unprecedented Growth.

Product Adaptation entails:

- customising products to meet the specific needs and preferences of local markets.
- modifying an existing product to make it more suitable for a new market.

This process ensures that products:

- resonate with local consumers
- comply with regulations
- stand out in competitive markets

Changing packaging, size, price or a brand itself make the product more appealing to foreign customers.

Product Adaptation Strategy

It's essential to understand the target market's cultural, social, and economic context.

It covers:

Cultural Sensitivity: Different cultures have unique tastes, preferences, and customs that influence purchasing behaviour.

Social Norms: Social norms and values can impact product acceptance.

Economic Factors: Products may need to be adapted to align with local income levels, offering more affordable options or premium versions as appropriate.

Regulatory Compliance

Ensuring compliance with these regulations is crucial for market entry and consumer trust.

Key areas in this regard include:

Product Standards: Adhering to local product standards may involve:

- specific materials
- manufacturing processes
- safety features

Labelling Requirements: Ensuring that product labels meet local requirements:

- language
- units of measurement
- mandatory information such as ingredients, nutritional facts, and safety warnings

Certification and Testing: Obtaining necessary certifications and conducting product testing to meet local regulatory standards.

Functional Adaptations

Products need functional changes to meet the practical needs of local consumers involving:

Climate Considerations: Adapting products to perform well under local climate conditions.

Usage Habits: Modifying products based on how they are used in different markets.

Aesthetic Adaptations: Aesthetic elements like design, colour, and packaging can significantly impact product appeal.

Aesthetic Adaptations involve:

Design Preferences: Understanding local design trends and preferences.

Packaging: Adapting packaging to suit local preferences and standards including changing the size, material, and design of packaging to enhance shelf appeal and functionality.

Effective Strategies for Product Development

Market-Driven Innovation: Innovation should be driven by a deep understanding of market needs and opportunities. This involves:

- **Market Research:** involving surveys, focus groups, and analysing consumer feedback.
- **Co-Creation:** helps ensure that new products resonate with the target market.

Incremental Innovation: Making small, continuous improvements to existing products.

This approach is cost-effective and reduces risk.

Radical Innovation: Developing entirely new products or significantly altering existing ones.

This approach can capture significant market share and differentiate the brand but involves higher risk and investment.

Leveraging Technology

Technology plays a crucial role in product development for international markets.

Key aspects include:

Digital Tools: Using digital tools and platforms for market research, product testing, and consumer feedback.

Sustainable Innovation: As consumers globally become more environmentally conscious, developing eco-friendly products can provide a competitive edge.

Product Formulation: Enhancing the product formulation to provide a natural glow and skin tone.

Marketing Messaging: Shifting the messaging to emphasise empowerment, confidence, and self-care.

Packaging and Branding: Updating packaging and branding to reflect the new positioning and appeal to a broader audience.

Wrapping Up

Adapting and developing products for international markets is essential to meet local preferences and regulatory requirements. This process ensures that products resonate with diverse consumer bases while maintaining brand consistency. Continuous innovation and responsiveness to market feedback are key to sustaining competitive advantage globally.

STRATEGY 7 MARKETING COMMUNICATIONS AND BRANDING

Crafting Powerful Marketing Communications and Branding for Global Impact.

Developing global brand strategies for building and maintaining a Global Brand Identity is quite essential for business promotion.

A strong global brand identity:

- enhances recognition
- fosters customer loyalty
- provides a competitive edge

Consistent Brand Messaging: Consistency in brand messaging is crucial for establishing a recognisable and trustworthy global brand.

This involves:

Unified Brand Vision: Develop a clear and compelling brand vision that resonates across different markets.

Standardised Visual Identity: Maintain a consistent visual identity, including logos, color schemes, typography, and packaging to create a cohesive brand image.

Cultural Adaptation: Adapt brand messages to fit local cultural nuances and preferences.

Understanding Local Markets

A global brand must resonate with local audiences.

Understanding the unique characteristics of each market is essential:

Market Research: Conduct thorough market research to understand local consumer behaviour, preferences, and trends.

Local Insights: Leverage local insights and expertise to create culturally relevant marketing campaigns.

Building Emotional Connections

Emotional connections with consumers enhance brand loyalty and advocacy.

Strategies to build emotional connections include:

Storytelling: Use storytelling to convey the brand's values, mission, and vision.

Brand Experiences: Create memorable brand experiences that engage consumers on an emotional level.

Customer Engagement: Foster engagement through social media, customer feedback, and personalised interactions.

Leveraging Digital Platforms

Digital platforms are vital for building a global brand.

Effective use of digital tools includes:

Social Media: Utilise social media platforms to connect with global audiences.

Content Marketing: Create high-quality, contents including blogs, videos, infographics, and user-generated content.

Influencer Partnerships: Collaborate with influencers who resonate with local audiences.

Key considerations for international advertising encompass:

Media Selection: Choose the right media channels based on local media consumption habits.

Localised Campaigns: Develop advertising campaigns that are culturally relevant and resonate with local audiences.

Cross-Channel Integration: Integrate advertising efforts across multiple channels for a cohesive and comprehensive approach.

Public Relations (PR)

PR helps build credibility and manage brand reputation in international markets.

Effective PR strategies incorporate:

Media Relations: Build relationships with local media outlets and journalists.

Provide them with compelling stories and press releases that highlight the brand's achievements and initiatives.

Events and Sponsorships: Sponsor local events to increase brand visibility and engage with the community.

Crisis Management: Develop a crisis management plan to address potential issues promptly and effectively.

Wrapping Up

Effective marketing communications and branding are vital for building brand identity and fostering customer loyalty. Clear, consistent messaging across channels enhances brand recognition and credibility.

A strong brand communicates value, differentiates from competitors, and creates emotional connections with consumers, driving long-term success.

STRATEGY 8
PRICING STRATEGIES

Price for Profit: Unlock the Secrets to Crafting Winning Pricing Strategies in Global Markets.

Price is the revenue-generating element of the marketing-mix.

It is of vital importance for the marketers to set the right price for two reasons:

- to match the buyer's perception
- to maximise profits

Connotation of Pricing Strategy

A pricing strategy attends for instrument deployed by the businesses to decide how much to charge for their goods and services. In the process, the interaction between price, margin and selling level is given specific consideration.

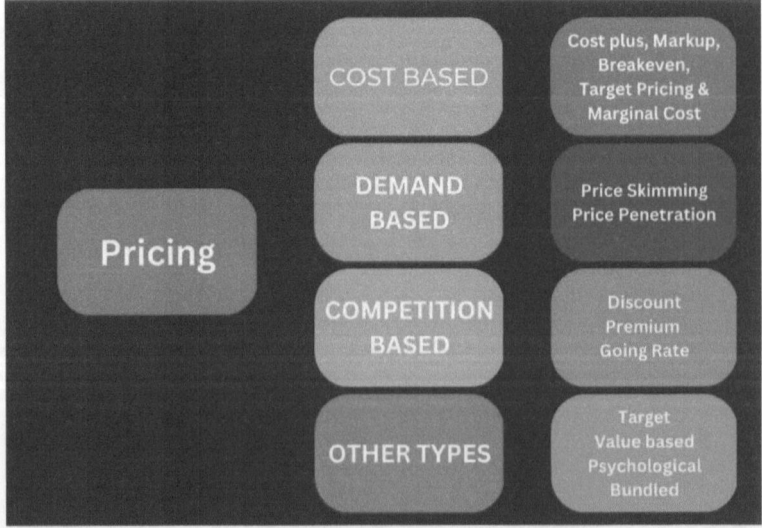

Key factors influencing international pricing include:

Cost Structure

- **Production Costs:** Production costs can vary significantly between countries due to differences in labour rates, availability of materials, and manufacturing efficiencies.

- **Shipping and Distribution:** Efficient logistics management is crucial to minimising these costs and maintaining profitability.

- **Tariffs and Taxes:** Import tariffs, value-added tax (VAT), and other local taxes can impact the final price of products in international markets.

- **Currency Fluctuations:** Companies need to monitor currency trends and use hedging strategies to mitigate the impact of unfavourable exchange rate movements on pricing.

Market Demand

- **Consumer Purchasing Power:** Products must be priced within the affordability range of the target audience while ensuring profitability.

- **Price Sensitivity:** Understanding how sensitive consumers in different markets are to price changes helps in setting optimal prices. In some markets, consumers may be highly price-sensitive. In others markets brand loyalty and perceived value might allow for premium pricing.

- **Competitive Landscape:** Competitive prices should be offered while differentiating your product based on quality, features, or brand value.
- **Market Positioning:** Your brand's positioning in the market influences pricing.
- **Pricing Models and Strategies:** The choice of Pricing strategy depends on factors such as market conditions, competition, and business objectives.

Selection of Ideal Pricing Strategy: Crucial Steps

- Conduct target market research
- Assess competitors' pricing
- Consider revenue model
- Get absolute clarity on costs
- Evaluate company's strengths and weaknesses
- Alignment with business USP

Role and Importance of Pricing Strategy

The effectiveness of Pricing Strategy on success of business is gauged by the facts that Pricing:

- inspires the target audience to purchase
- portrays the true value of the brand
- instills confidence in the customer for product or service

Popular Pricing Models and Strategies

1. Penetration Pricing

Definition

Entering the market at a low price and eventually increasing the price.

The objective of Penetration Pricing Strategy is to attract buyers by offering lower prices on goods and services than competitors. This strategy can help increase:

- brand awareness and loyalty
- long-term contracts
- drive profits

After penetrating a market, business owners can increase prices to better reflect the status of the product's position within the market.

Suitability: Small businesses aim at building brand loyalty and reputation.

Benefits:

- Quick adoption and acceptance by customers.
- Generation of high sales.
- Creation of large inventory turnover.
- Boost to positive word of mouth.

Drawbacks:

- Can create pricing expectations for customers.
- Customers will be bargain hunters.
- Can trigger price wars.
- Customers could perceive discounted products as cheap or bad quality thereby hurting brand image.

2. Economy Pricing

Definition

Pricing a product low because of low costs of production, marketing, and advertising, and relying on high sales volume to generate profit.

Economy pricing aims to attract the most price-conscious consumers.

It involves minimising marketing and production expenses.

Companies can set a lower sales price and still turn a slight profit.

Suitability:

Small businesses desirous of keeping overhead costs low.

Benefits:

- Easy implementation.
- Low customer acquisition costs.
- Attracts price-sensitive customers.

- Best strategy for an economic downturn or recession.

Drawbacks:

- Cutting production costs can be challenging.
- Works only if there is a steady stream of customers.
- Potential to negatively impact brand perception.

3. Premium Pricing

Definition

Pricing a product deliberately high to encourage favourable perceptions of the brand based on the price.

With premium pricing, businesses set costs higher because they have a unique product or brand that no one can compete with. This strategy is appropriate with a considerable competitive advantage.

Business owners should ensure that the product's packaging, the store's decor, and the marketing strategy support the premium price.

Suitability:

Small businesses enjoy considerable competitive advantage.

Benefits:

- Improves desirability of brand.
- Higher profit margins.
- Provides a competitive advantage.

Drawbacks:

- Higher cost of production and marketing.
- Smaller target audience.
- Reduced sales volume.

4. Price Skimming

Definition

Setting new product prices high and subsequently lowering the price as competitors enter the market.

Price skimming is designed to help businesses maximise sales of new products and services. This involves setting rates high during the initial phase of a product introduction.

Prices are gradually lowered with the entry of competitors.

Suitability:

Small businesses having products that are in high demand.

Benefits:

- Allows businesses to maximise profits through early adopters.
- Easy to recoup development costs.
- Creates an illusion of exclusivity and quality.

Drawbacks:

- Creation of excess inventory.

- The quality of the new service or product must justify the higher cost to be effective.
- Fails to work if competitors are creating similar products.
- Simplifies the decision-making process for customers.

5. Value Pricing

Definition

Pricing a product based on how much the customer believes it's worth.

Value pricing implies setting prices based on the customer's perceived value of what is offered. This occurs when external factors, like a sharp increase in competition or a recession, encourage the small business to further provide additional value to its customers to maintain sales.

This strategy recognises that customers ignore product costs so long as the consumer derives an excellent value with the purchase.

Suitability:

Small businesses specialising in SaaS or subscriptions.

Benefits:

- Potential for high profit margins.
- Increased perceived value in brand and services.
- Increased customer loyalty.

Drawbacks:

- Warrants additional market research to determine value to target audience.
- Markets tend to be very niche being high-end.
- More cost of production.

6. Dynamic Pricing

Definition

Pricing varies based on marketing and customer demand.

Under Dynamic pricing different prices are charged depending on who is buying the product or service or when it is bought. It is a flexible pricing strategy that takes many factors into account—particularly demand and supply.

Dynamic pricing is also called:

- Demand pricing
- Surge pricing
- Time-based pricing

The greatest risk emerges when variable prices are applied to products or services that are typically bought by price-sensitive customers.

Suitability:

Small businesses looking to maximise their profit margins and boost declining sales.

Benefits:

- Pricing reflects the market demand for the product or service.
- Provides more insight into customer demand and purchase patterns.
- Helps to maximise profits by matching price to the demand.

Drawbacks:

- Customers may be scared of fluctuating prices.
- Higher risk of price wars.
- Increases competition within the industry.

7. Competitive Pricing

Definition

Pricing products based on the price of competitive products, rather than cost or target profit, usually cheaper than competitors.

Competitive pricing is when prices match those of similar products that are sold by competitors.

It involves selling products or services at a better price.

It can be choosen to offer better payment terms.

Suitability:

Small businesses that are just starting out.

Benefits:

- Simple implementation.
- Can be combined with other strategies such as cost-plus pricing to make efforts more rewarding.

Drawbacks:

- Not good to use long-term since competitors will catch on and modify their strategy.
- Not a strategy to use if you want to stand out.

8. Cost-Plus Pricing

Definition:

Adding a fixed percentage on top of the cost of producing a product, regardless of consumer demand or competitors' pricing.

Cost-plus pricing is a strategy of marking up (adding a fixed percentage) the cost of services and goods to arrive at your selling price.

We can include fixed and variable costs that will be incurred in manufacturing products. Then add the mark-up percentage to that cost. This strategy is widely used since it is fair and non-discriminatory.

Suitability:

Small businesses with a cost advantage.

Also, in using price transparency as a differentiator.

Benefits:

- May result in positive differentiation and customer trust.
- Reduced risk of price wars.
- Can provide predictable profits.
- Simple implementation.

Drawbacks:

- Discourages efficiency and cost containment.
- Customers can perceive the product negatively.
- Much of the calculation is an estimation.
- Can be difficult to change prices when needed.

9. Freemium Pricing

Definition:

Offering a product for free alongside paid versions with more features.

Under Freemium pricing strategy a service or product is given to a customer free of charge unless they want to access premium features or services within that product.

Suitability:

Small businesses that intend to offer both free and paid versions of their product, and those that offer free trials.

Benefits:

- Potential to unlock viral growth.

- Creates a no-risk environment that attracts customers who want to try something for free.
- Opportunity to monetise on advertising.

Drawbacks:

- A majority of free users may never convert.
- Cash reserves can be depleted quickly because of a large number of non-paying users.
- May require additional customer service support for freemium users, which can be costly.

Wrapping Up

Pricing strategies must balance profitability with market demand and competitive positioning. By considering factors such as cost, value perception, and market conditions, businesses can set prices that attract customers while sustaining margins. Strategic pricing is essential for market entry, product positioning, and overall business growth.

- Penetration Pricing
- Economy Pricing Pricing
- Premium Pricing
- Penetration Pricing
- Price Skimming
- Value Pricing
- Dynamic Pricing
- Competitive Pricing
- Cost-Plus Pricing

STRATEGY 9
DISTRIBUTION CHANNELS AND SUPPLY CHAIN MANAGEMENT

Go Beyond Borders: Proven Distribution Tactics to Reach Customers Worldwide.

The choice of appropriate distribution channels can impact:

- market penetration
- brand visibility
- customer satisfaction
- overall business success

Key Types of Distribution Channels

Direct Channels: Selling directly to consumers through company-owned stores, websites, or sales teams.

Indirect Channels: Utilising intermediaries such as wholesalers, distributors, and retailers to reach consumers.

Hybrid Channels: Combining direct and indirect channels to leverage the benefits of both approaches.

Evaluating Market Characteristics: Main Factors

Market Size and Density: Large, densely populated markets may benefit from direct channels such as online sales, while smaller, fragmented markets may require multiple intermediaries.

Consumer Preferences: Understanding local shopping habits and preferences helps in selecting channels that align with consumer behaviour.

Infrastructure and Logistics: In regions with well-developed logistics networks, direct distribution may be feasible, whereas in areas with limited infrastructure, local distributors may be necessary.

Analysing Channel Capabilities

Evaluating the capabilities of potential distribution partners is critical for ensuring effective market coverage.

Consider the following factors in this context:

Experience and Expertise: Experienced partners can provide valuable insights and help navigate market challenges.

Network Reach: A partner with extensive coverage can enhance market penetration.

Reputation and Reliability: Reliable partners ensure timely delivery and high customer satisfaction.

Selecting the Right Channels

Based on the evaluation, select the most appropriate distribution channels for your product and market.

The choice should align with your overall business strategy and objectives.

Common Channel Strategies

Direct-to-Consumer (DTC): Ideal for businesses with strong brand recognition and online presence. DTC channels include company-owned stores, websites, and social media platforms.

Retail Partnerships: Collaborating with established retailers can provide immediate market access and brand visibility. This strategy is suitable for consumer goods and high-traffic markets.

Distributor Networks: Leveraging local distributors can be effective in markets with complex logistics or regulatory environments. Distributors handle warehousing, logistics, and local marketing efforts.

Franchising and Licensing: Expanding through franchising or licensing agreements allows for rapid market entry with lower investment.

Meaning of Supply Chain

Supply Chain involves the process that creates systems which make people, resources, information and organisations work together to move products and services from the suppliers to consumers.

Supply Chain Optimisation

Effective supply chain management :
- enhances product availability
- reduces costs

- improves customer satisfaction

Key components of supply chain optimisation

Supply Chain Planning

Supply chain planning involves forecasting demand, planning inventory levels, and coordinating production schedules.

Key steps include:

- **Demand Forecasting:** Accurate forecasting helps in maintaining optimal inventory levels and minimising stock outs or excess inventory.

- **Inventory Management:** Proper inventory management reduces holding costs and ensures product availability.

- **Production Planning:** Coordinating production schedules with demand forecasts to optimize manufacturing processes.

Logistics and Transportation

Efficient logistics and transportation are critical for timely and cost-effective delivery of products.

Key considerations include:

- **Transportation Modes:** Selecting the appropriate transportation modes -air, sea, rail, road- based on cost, speed, and reliability.

- **Carrier Selection:** Evaluate carriers based on their service quality, network reach, and cost-effectiveness.

- **Route Optimisation:** Route optimisation considers factors such as distance, traffic conditions, and delivery schedules.

Warehousing and Distribution

Efficient warehousing and distribution are essential for managing inventory and fulfilling customer orders.

Key strategies include:

- **Warehouse Location:** Consider proximity to key markets, suppliers, and transportation hubs.

- **Warehouse Management Systems (WMS):** Implementing WMS to automate and streamline warehouse operations, including inventory tracking, order picking, and shipping. WMS improves accuracy and efficiency.

- **Cross-Docking:** Cross-docking reduces inventory holding costs and speeds up delivery.

Technology and Innovation

Leveraging technology and innovation is crucial for optimising the supply chain.

Key technologies include:

- **Blockchain:** Blockchain enhances traceability, reduces fraud, and improves data accuracy.

- **Internet of Things (IoT):** IoT provides valuable data for predictive maintenance and proactive supply chain management.

- **Artificial Intelligence (AI):** Employing AI for demand forecasting, route optimisation, and inventory management. AI-driven insights help in making data-informed decisions and improving supply chain efficiency.

Wrapping Up

Efficient distribution channels and supply chain management ensure that products reach the right customers at the right time. Streamlined logistics, strong partnerships, and technology integration are key to minimising costs and enhancing customer satisfaction. An optimised supply chain supports business scalability and responsiveness to market changes.

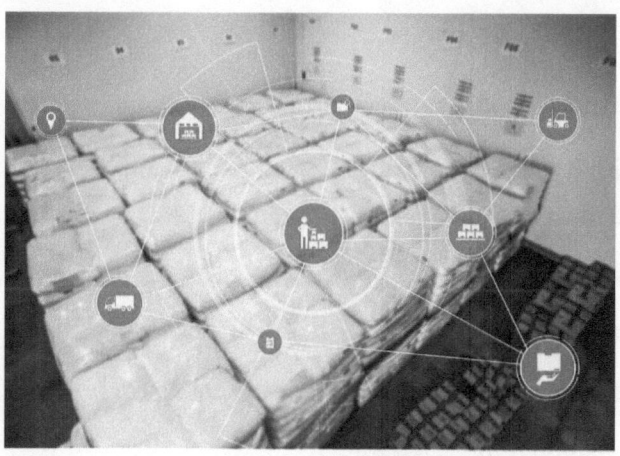

CHAPTER 10
LEVERAGING DIGITAL MARKETING

Go Digital, Go Global: Harness the Power of Digital Marketing to Expand Your Reach Worldwide.

Digital Revolution - Here to Stay

Digital marketing has emerged as a bedrock of strategic international marketing in today's globalised economy.

The proliferation of internet access and mobile technology has rendered tremendous assistance to businesses who can now reach and engage with customers across the globe with unprecedented ease and precision.

This digital revolution has transformed the traditional marketing landscape, enabling companies to harness:

- data-driven insights
- leverage social media platforms
- deploy targeted advertising campaigns that resonate with diverse international audiences

A robust Digital Marketing Strategy is a vital component for businesses aiming to:

- expand their international footprint
- enhance brand visibility

- drive sustainable growth

Connotation of Digital Marketing Strategies

Digital marketing strategies refer to the comprehensive plans and tactics that businesses employ to promote their products or services using digital channels and technologies.

These strategies aim to reach and engage with target audiences through various digital platforms such as websites, search engines, social media, email, mobile apps.

Objectives of Digital Marketing

- Increasing brand awareness
- Driving website traffic
- Leads generation
- Boosting online sales
- Improving customer retention
- Enhancement of brand reputation

Be Careful: Digital Marketing Mistakes to Avoid

In the process of targeting a global audience, some crucial digital marketing mistakes need to be avoided to achieve success and ensure corrective actions.

Lack of focus: Concentrate on finding the right marketing techniques for your desired audience and create measurable goals to track over time.

Overlooking the interest of the target audience: Building customer personas can help ensure you direct efforts towards the right market.

Not optimising your site for mobile: If your website is not optimised for mobile, there is a risk of missing out on potential customers.

Not using social proof: Testimonials help your company build trust and credibility with new consumers.

Trying too many things at once: It is vital to find the best digital mode-from email, social media and SEO-for your objective and proceed slowly, scaling up over time.

Major Digital Marketing Strategies for Application

Search Engine Optimisation (SEO): The process of optimising a website to rank higher in search engine results pages, organically driving more traffic and visibility.

Pay-per-Click (PPC) Advertising: Displaying ads on search engines or other platforms and paying only when users click on the ads.

Content Marketing: Creating and distributing valuable and relevant content to attract and engage the target audience through blog posts, videos, infographics, and so on.

Social Media Marketing: Leveraging social media platforms by creating and sharing content, running paid ads, and interacting with followers.

Email Marketing: Utilising email to send targeted messages and promotions to a subscriber list. This strategy helps nurture leads, build relationships with customers, and drive conversions.

Influencer Marketing: This strategy leverages the influencers' credibility and reach to increase brand visibility.

Mobile Marketing: Optimising marketing efforts for mobile devices, including mobile-friendly websites, mobile apps, and SMS marketing.

Conversion Rate Optimisation (CRO): Analysing and optimising various elements of a website or landing page to increase the conversion rate and improve user experience.

Significant Role Digital Marketing in Business Promotion

Contribution of Digital Marketing Strategy to boosting strategic international marketing is easily reflected in the following aspects:

Global Reach and Market Penetration

Wide Audience Access: Digital marketing enables small businesses to reach a global audience without the need for physical presence in each market.

Worldwide Targeting: Social media platforms, search engines, and email marketing can target customers worldwide.

24/7 Online Presence: Websites and social media profiles ensure that businesses are accessible to potential customers at any time, regardless of time zones.

Cost-Effective Marketing

Lower Costs: Digital marketing campaigns, such as pay-per-click (PPC) ads, social media ads, and email marketing, require less investment compared to traditional marketing methods like print and TV ads.

High ROI: A high return on investment (ROI) can be achieved with well-optimised digital campaigns because of precise targeting and tracking capabilities.

Targeted Advertising and Personalisation

Precise Targeting: Digital marketing tools allow businesses to target specific demographics, geographic locations, and interests, ensuring that marketing efforts reach the most relevant audience.

Personalisation: Businesses can personalise marketing messages to individual customer preferences, enhancing engagement and conversion rates.

Enhanced Customer Engagement and Interaction

Social Media Engagement: Platforms like Facebook, Instagram, LinkedIn, and Twitter enable direct interaction with customers, fostering relationships and brand loyalty.

Content Marketing: Blogs, videos, and other content types provide valuable information to customers.

Data-Driven Decision Making

Analytics and Insights: Digital marketing provides access to real-time data and analytics enabling businesses to track and understand customer behaviours, and make informed decisions.

Continuous Improvement: By analysing campaign metrics, businesses can continuously refine their strategies for better results.

Flexibility and Scalability

Adaptable Strategies: Digital marketing campaigns can be quickly adjusted based on performance data, allowing businesses to respond to market changes and trends.

Scalability: Successful campaigns can be scaled to larger audiences or additional markets with relative ease, supporting business growth.

Enhanced Brand Awareness and Positioning

Global Brand Building: Consistent digital marketing efforts help build brand awareness on a global scale.

Positioning: Digital marketing allows small businesses to position themselves effectively against competitors by highlighting unique value propositions and differentiators.

Improved Customer Experience and Satisfaction

Customer Service: Digital platforms provide channels for customer support and feedback.

CRM Integration: Customer relationship management (CRM) systems can be integrated with digital marketing tools to enhance customer experience through personalised communication and offers.

Developing Digital Marketing Strategies : A Step- by - Process

- **Setting SMART GOALS**- specific, measurable, attainable, relevant, and time-bound.

- **Aligning objectives with overall business strategy:** Consider how your digital marketing efforts will support and contribute to the growth and expansion of your business in international markets.

- **Set market-specific goals and metrics:** Each international market may have unique characteristics and dynamics that require specific goals and metrics.

- **Conduct market research:** Tailor your goals and metrics to align with the local market conditions and business objectives.

- **Identifying popular platforms:** Social media platforms and search engines in target markets serve the marketing purpose effectively.

- **Consider demography:** User demographics, market penetration, and engagement levels on different platforms serve the purpose .

- **Local preferences and cultural nuances in channel selection:** Take into account the local preferences, cultural nuances, and communication styles of each target market when selecting digital channels.

- **Adapt your digital marketing channels:** Consider working with local marketing experts or agencies to gain insights into the cultural nuances and preferences of each market.

- **Adapting content**: Messaging for different markets.

- **Localising:** Website and landing pages.

Wrapping up

A well-crafted digital marketing strategy is indispensable for businesses seeking to thrive in the competitive arena of international markets.

By committing to a strategic and data-driven approach to digital marketing, your business can unlock significant opportunities for growth and success on the international stage.

Digital marketing is a powerful tool for reaching and engaging global audiences with precision and efficiency. By leveraging data analytics, social media, SEO, and content marketing, businesses can create targeted campaigns that drive brand awareness and conversions. Continuous innovation in digital strategies is essential to stay ahead in a rapidly evolving landscape.

STRATEGY 11
CUSTOMER RELATIONSHIP MANAGEMENT (CRM)

Build Loyalty Across Borders: How Effective CRM Can Turn Global Customers into Lifelong Advocates.
Role of CRM in Business

Customer Relationship Management (CRM) is a strategic approach that combines practices, strategies, and technologies used by companies to manage and analyse customer interactions and data throughout the customer lifecycle.

In today's highly globalised business environment, the ability to manage and nurture customer relationships across diverse markets has become a critical determinant of success.

As companies expand beyond their home markets, they encounter varying customer behaviours, cultural nuances, and regulatory landscapes that require a sophisticated and adaptable approach to customer relationship management (CRM).

An effective international CRM strategy:

- helps businesses streamline operations
- enhances customer experiences
- serves as a powerful tool for building brand loyalty
- drives sustained growth in the global marketplace

By leveraging technology, data, and cultural insights, organisations can develop CRM strategies that resonate with customers worldwide, ensuring that they remain competitive and relevant in an ever-evolving market landscape.

Meaning of CRM

Customer Relationship Management (CRM) is the most viable and efficient approach to creating and nurturing relationships with customers.

- CRM caters to past, present, and prospective clientele.
- CRM encourages solid personal bonding with customers.

In the process, the business is elevated to the next level of success!

A Customer Relationship Management (CRM) is a strategic approach that integrates:

- processes
- technology
- human resources
- to enhance the relationships a company has with its customers

In the context of international marketing, CRM strategies must account for:

- diverse markets

- cultural differences
- varying customer behaviours

Types of CRM Solutions

CRM systems typically consist of several key components that work together to enhance customer interaction and experience:

Operational CRM

Operational CRM focuses on automating and streamlining customer-facing processes. This includes:

- sales automation
- marketing automation
- service automation

It enables businesses to manage their day-to-day activities such as:

- lead management
- contact management
- campaign management
- customer support

Analytical CRM

Analytical CRM involves the analysis of customer data collected through various sources. It uses:

- data mining

- pattern recognition
- predictive modelling

to gain insights into customer behaviours and preferences.

These insights help businesses make:
- informed decisions
- tailor their marketing efforts
- enhance customer satisfaction

Collaborative CRM

Collaborative CRM facilitates collaboration between different departments within an organisation and between the organisation and its external partners, such as suppliers and distributors.

It ensures that all parts of the company work together to provide a unified customer experience.

Strategic CRM

Strategic CRM is focused on developing long-term customer relationships. It involves:
- understanding customer needs
- behaviours
- preferences to create value propositions

that are beneficial for both the customer and the company.

This component is closely aligned with the overall business strategy and helps in building customer loyalty.

Primary Goals of CRM

- improve customer service relationships
- assist in customer retention
- drive sales growth

By using a CRM system, businesses can:

- streamline processes
- build stronger relationships with customers
- increase profitability

International CRM Strategy: Key Components

1. Understanding Cultural Differences

- **Cultural Sensitivity:** Recognise and respect the cultural norms, values, and traditions of each market.
- **Localised Communication:** Tailor messages to resonate with local cultures and languages.
- **Cultural Training:** Equip your team with knowledge about the cultures they are engaging with to avoid missteps and build trust.

2. Customer Segmentation

- **Demographic Segmentation:** Group customers by age, gender, income, education, and occupation.
- **Geographic Segmentation:** Divide the market based on regions, countries, cities, or neighbourhoods.
- **Psychographic Segmentation:** Segment customers based on lifestyle, values, attitudes, and interests.
- **Behavioural Segmentation:** Classify customers based on their behaviour, usage, and purchasing patterns.

3. Data Collection and Management

- **Centralised Data Repository:** Implement a robust CRM system that consolidates customer data from all touch-points.
- **Data Privacy Compliance:** Ensure adherence to international data protection regulations (e.g., GDPR, CCPA).
- **Real-Time Data Analysis:** Utilise analytics tools to gain real-time insights into customer behaviour and preferences.

4. Personalisation

- **Customised Marketing Campaigns:** Develop personalised marketing campaigns based on customer data and preferences.

- **Tailored Product Offerings:** Adjust product offerings to meet the specific needs and desires of different market segments.

- **Personalised Customer Service:** Provide customer service that is responsive and tailored to individual customer needs.

5. Technology Integration

- **CRM Software:** Implement CRM software that supports multiple languages and currencies.

- **Marketing Automation:** Use automation tools to streamline marketing efforts and enhance customer engagement.

- **Social Media Integration:** Leverage social media platforms to engage with customers and gather feedback.

6. Customer Engagement

- **Multi-Channel Communication:** Engage customers through various channels including email, social media, mobile apps, and in-store interactions.

- **Loyalty Programs:** Develop loyalty programs that reward customers for their continued business and engagement.

- **Customer Feedback Systems:** Implement systems for collecting and analysing customer feedback to continuously improve products and services.

7. Performance Measurement

- **KPIs and Metrics:** Establish key performance indicators (KPIs) and metrics to measure the success of CRM initiatives.
- **Customer Lifetime Value (CLV):** Calculate CLV to understand the long-term value of customers.
- **Customer Satisfaction and Retention Rates:** Monitor customer satisfaction and retention rates to assess the effectiveness of CRM strategies.

Implementation of International CRM Strategy

1. Assessment and Planning

- Conduct a thorough market analysis to understand the target audience in each region.
- Develop a detailed CRM strategy that aligns with the company's overall business objectives.

2. Technology Selection and Integration

- Choose a CRM platform that supports international operations.
- Integrate the CRM system with existing marketing, sales, and customer service tools.

3. Training and Development

- Train employees on the CRM system and the importance of cultural sensitivity.

- Develop ongoing training programs to keep the team updated on CRM best practices.

4. Data Management

- Implement robust data collection and management practices.
- Ensure compliance with international data protection laws.

5. Customer Engagement Initiatives

- Launch targeted marketing campaigns to engage customers in different regions.
- Implement loyalty programs and personalised customer service initiatives.

6. Continuous Improvement

- Regularly review CRM performance metrics.
- Gather customer feedback and use it to make continuous improvements to CRM strategies.

Benefits of CRM

Implementing a CRM system provides several benefits, especially in an international context:

1. Enhanced Customer Satisfaction

By centralising customer information and providing a holistic view of the customer, CRM systems enable businesses to offer personalised services, which lead to increased customer satisfaction and loyalty.

2. Improved Efficiency and Productivity

CRM automates routine tasks, such as data entry and follow-up emails, freeing up employees to focus on more strategic activities.

This leads to improved efficiency and productivity within the organisation.

3. Better Decision-Making

With access to real-time customer data and advanced analytics, businesses can make data-driven decisions.

This helps in identifying trends, predicting customer needs, and improving overall business strategies.

4. Increased Sales

CRM systems help in identifying and nurturing leads, managing the sales pipeline, and closing deals more effectively.

The ability to cross-sell and upsell based on customer data also contributes to increased sales.

5. Effective Marketing

By segmenting customers and understanding their preferences, businesses can create targeted marketing campaigns that resonate with specific customer groups. This leads to higher conversion rates and better return on investment (ROI) for marketing efforts.

6. Enhanced Customer Retention

CRM enables businesses to track customer interactions and identify potential issues before they escalate. By addressing customer concerns proactively, businesses can improve customer retention and reduce churn rates.

"It is not your Customers' Job to remember you. It is your Obligation and Responsibility to make sure they don't have a chance to forget you"

- Patricia Fripp

Challenges and Considerations

Data Privacy and Security

- Navigating varying data privacy laws across different countries.
- Ensuring data security to protect customer information.

Cultural Diversity

- Managing the complexity of catering to diverse cultural preferences and expectations.
- Ensuring effective communication across language barriers.

Adoption

- Overcoming resistance to new technology among employees.
- Ensuring seamless integration of CRM systems with existing tools and processes.

Scalability

- Designing a CRM strategy that can scale with the company's growth in international markets.
- Managing the increased complexity of data and customer interactions as the business expands.

Wrapping Up

A well-crafted CRM strategy is more than just a tool for managing customer interactions. It is the backbone of successful international marketing.

As businesses navigate the complexities of operating in diverse markets, the importance of a strategic, localised, and customer-centric approach cannot be overstated.

From understanding and segmenting global customers to ensuring data compliance and fostering meaningful relationships, CRM strategies tailored to international.

CRM systems are vital for building and maintaining strong customer relationships, enabling personalised interactions and improved customer service.

By centralising customer data, businesses can better understand customer needs, predict behaviour, and enhance loyalty. Effective CRM drives customer satisfaction and long-term business success.

STRATEGY 12
KPIS AND PERFORMANCE MEASUREMENT

Measure What Matters: Unlock Global Success with the Right KPIs and Performance Metrics.

Strategy for Marketing KPIs: Measuring Performance and Improvement

In today's competitive business environment businesses are required to ensure that marketing efforts are-well-executed and impactful.

It is essential to implement a comprehensive strategy for measuring performance through Key Performance Indicators (KPIs).

Marketing KPIs are measurable values that demonstrate how effectively a company is achieving key marketing objectives.

Marketing KPIs provide a clear and quantitative way to gauge the success of marketing activities, making it possible to identify areas for improvement and to refine strategies over time.

Role and Importance of Marketing KPIs

Marketing KPIs serve multiple purposes:

- offer a benchmark for success, allowing businesses to set realistic goals and track progress against them.
- provide insights into customer behaviour, market trends, and the effectiveness of marketing channels and tactics.
- enable continuous improvement by highlighting what works and what doesn't, allowing for data-driven decision-making.
- foster accountability within marketing teams, ensuring that all efforts align with broader business objectives.

Setting the Right KPIs

The foundation of any successful KPI strategy is selecting the right metrics to track.

The key is to choose KPIs that are directly aligned with your marketing goals.

A list of Right KPIS runs as under:

Lead Generation

- **Number of Leads:** Total number of leads generated within a given period.
- **Cost per Lead (CPL):** The average cost of acquiring a lead.

- **Conversion Rate:** Percentage of leads that convert into customers.

Brand Awareness:

- **Impressions:** Number of times your content is displayed to users.
- **Reach:** Number of unique users who see your content.
- **Brand Mentions:** Number of times your brand is mentioned online.

Customer Acquisition:

- **Customer Acquisition Cost (CAC):** Total cost of acquiring a new customer.
- **Customer Lifetime Value (CLTV):** Total revenue a business can expect from a single customer account.

Engagement:

- **Click-Through Rate (CTR):** Percentage of people who click on a link or ad after seeing it.
- **Bounce Rate:** Percentage of visitors who leave a website after viewing only one page.
- **Social Media Engagement:** Likes, shares, comments, and overall interaction with social media content.

Sales Performance:

- **Sales Revenue:** Total income generated from sales.
- **Sales Growth:** Percentage increase in sales over a specific period.
- **Market Share:** Percentage of an industry's total sales that is earned by your company.

Implementing a Measurement Framework

As a sequel to selection of KPIs , the next step is to establish a measurement framework. This involves:

1. Setting Baselines: Determine the current performance level for each KPI to establish a benchmark against which future performance can be measured.

2. Defining Targets: Set specific, measurable, achievable, relevant, and time-bound (SMART) targets for each KPI. These targets should be challenging yet realistic and should reflect the overall marketing strategy.

3. Data Collection: Implement systems for collecting and analysing data. This could involve using tools like Google Analytics, CRM systems, social media analytics, and marketing automation platforms.

Ensure that data collection is consistent and accurate.

4. Regular Reporting: Establish a regular reporting schedule, such as weekly, monthly, or quarterly reports, depending on the nature of the KPIs and the business cycle. Reports should include data on current performance, comparisons with past performance, and analysis of trends.

5. Continuous Review and Adjustment: KPIs should be regularly reviewed and adjusted based on changes in the market, business objectives, or marketing tactics. This is to ensure that marketing efforts remain aligned with business goals and respond to new opportunities and challenges.

Interpreting KPI Data

Interpreting KPI data involves understanding the context, trends, and anomalies that may impact performance.

Analyse Trends: Look at data over time to identify patterns or trends.

- Are there seasonal fluctuations?
- Has there been consistent growth or decline?

Contextualise Data: Investigate Anomalies: Sudden spikes or drops in KPIs should be investigated to understand the cause. This could involve looking at external factors, such as market conditions, or internal factors, such as changes in strategy or execution.

Optimising Marketing Performance

To optimise marketing performance use the insights gained from KPIs to make informed decisions that enhance marketing effectiveness.

Strategies for optimisation include:

- **A/B Testing:** Experiment with different versions of marketing materials (e.g., email campaigns, landing pages, ads) to see which performs better.

- **Personalisation:** Tailor marketing messages and offers to specific customer segments to increase relevance and engagement.

- **Channel Optimisation:** Focus on the most effective marketing channels by reallocating resources from underperforming channels to those that yield the highest returns.

- **Content Strategy:** Use insights from KPIs to refine content strategies, focusing on topics and formats that resonate most with your audience.

Wrapping Up

A comprehensive strategy for marketing KPIs is essential for any business looking to maximise the impact of its marketing efforts.

By implementing a robust measurement framework, businesses can measure their marketing performance and also drive continuous improvement.

This approach ensures that marketing efforts are not only effective in the short term but also contribute to long-term business success.

Key Performance Indicators (KPIs) are essential for tracking progress towards business goals and optimising strategies. By regularly measuring performance across key metrics, businesses can make data-driven decisions, identify areas for improvement, and ensure alignment with objectives. Continuous performance monitoring is crucial for achieving sustained success.

PART 9
TACTICAL MOVES

"Expanding globally is not just about scale; it's about creating meaningful content that resonates with people from diverse backgrounds. At The Huffington Post, we focus on stories that connect with the human experience, transcending cultural and geographical boundaries."

- Arianna Huffington, Founder of The Huffington Post

CHAPTER 10
3Ts STRATEGY

Crack the Code of International Markets: Strategies to Scale Your Brand Globally.

Tips+Tricks and Tactics

In today's globalised economy, mastering the art of international marketing has become the necessity for businesses seeking to thrive on the world stage. The businesses are essentially confronted with:

- complexities of entering new markets
- navigating cultural differences
- effectively communicating brand's value proposition

Such a scenario warrants formulation of robust strategy of international marketing.

Here we delve into the powerful 3 Ts Strategy. It comprises Tips, Tricks and Tactics that can help you craft successful international marketing strategies.

They serve the purpose of both the small business aiming to expand its reach or an established brand looking to strengthen its global presence. These insights will equip you with the knowledge to achieve your goals and compete confidently across borders.

Tips + Tricks and Tactics for Strategic International marketing tailored for small businesses run as:

1. Understand the Target Market

- **Market Research:** Conduct thorough market research to understand the cultural, economic, and legal landscape of the target country.
Identify key customer preferences, buying behaviours, and local competitors.

- **Customer Segmentation:** Segment your international audience based on demographics, psychographics, and cultural factors to tailor your marketing efforts effectively.

2. Localise Your Brand

- **Cultural Sensitivity:** Adapt your brand messaging, imagery, and tone to resonate with the local culture. Avoid direct translations. Instead , it's better to localise content to reflect the nuances of the local language and culture.

- **Product Adaptation:** Modify your product or service offerings to meet local tastes, preferences, or regulations.

3. Leverage Digital Marketing Channels

- **Social Media Marketing:** Utilise popular social media platforms in the target country to build brand awareness and engage with local customers. Tailor your content strategy to the platform's user base.

- **Search Engine Optimisation (SEO):** Optimise your website and content for local search engines.

4. Build Strong Local Partnerships

- **Distribution Channels:** Collaborate with local distributors, agents, or retailers who understand the market and can help navigate regulatory requirements and distribution logistics.

- **Strategic Alliances:** Form partnerships with local businesses, influencers, or organisations to enhance credibility and gain market insights.

5. Comply with Local Regulations

- **Legal Compliance:** Understand and comply with local laws and regulations related to marketing, advertising, product labeling, and data protection. This includes understanding tariffs, taxes, and import/export regulations.

- **Intellectual Property Protection:** Protect your brand and intellectual property in the international market by registering trademarks and patents in the target country.

6. Create a Competitive Pricing Strategy

- **Currency Fluctuations:** Consider currency exchange rates and their impact on pricing. Adjust your pricing strategy to remain competitive while maintaining profitability.

- **Value Proposition:** Emphasise the unique value your product or service offers compared to local competitors -in terms of quality, innovation, or customer service.

7. Monitor and Adapt

- **Continuous Feedback Loop:** To refine your strategies establish a system to regularly gather feedback from international customers and partners.

- **Agility:** Be prepared to quickly adapt your marketing strategies based on market trends, customer feedback, and competitive pressures.

8. Invest in Cross-Cultural Training

- **Team Training:** Ensure your team is equipped with the cultural knowledge and communication skills needed to interact effectively with international customers and partners.

- **Cultural Immersion:** Try to spend time in the target market to gain first hand experience and insights into local customs and business practices.

9. Utilise Data Analytics

- **Customer Insights:** Leverage data analytics to track the performance of your international marketing campaigns strategies.

- **Market Trends:** Stay informed about global market trends and economic indicators that could impact your business in international markets.

10. Be Patient and Persistent

- **Long-Term Perspective:** Be patient and persistent in your efforts, and focus on long-term growth rather than short-term gains.

- **Learning from Mistakes:** Adjust your strategies based on what works and what doesn't, and keep moving forward.

By following these **Tips, Tricks and Tactics,** small businesses can navigate the complexities of international marketing and build a successful global presence.

Wrapping Up

Successfully navigating the intricate landscape of international marketing is both an art and a science. By leveraging the right strategies - it is possible to position your brand for global success.

It should always be borne in mind that the key to international marketing lies in being adaptable, culturally aware, and innovative.

Application of 3 Ts Strategy of Tips, Tricks and Tactics can substantially help you to expand your market reach.

You will positively succeed in building lasting connections with diverse audiences worldwide. This will go a long way to ensure that your business remains competitive. Its resilience in an ever-changing global landscape will stand you in good stead.

CHAPTER 11

FROM BLUNDERS TO BRILLIANCE: A STORY OF GLOBE - TROTTING

Dear Readers,

This interesting Anecdote amply illustrates:

- Understanding the target audience without underestimating their intelligence ensures marketing success.

- Essence of Cultural and Social Sensitivity has to be mastered for success in International Marketing.

Once upon a time, in a bustling marketing agency, there were two bright young marketers named Mohan and Sohan. They were known for their creative ideas and bold campaigns that had won the hearts of many in their home country.

One day, their boss called them into his office with a new challenge:

"Mohan and Sohan , it's time for you to take your talents global!"

Excited by the prospect of international success, they eagerly accepted the task.

But little did they know, the road to global glory was paved with cultural twists and turns.

By the way, Mohan is more impulsive, quick to act.

Sohan is more cautious and research-driven.

Their journey ran through the Stages and they had varied lessons to learn on the way.

Lesson 1: The Tomato Sauce Debacle

Their first campaign was for a popular tomato sauce brand. "Simple enough," thought Mohan "We'll call it 'Canned

Freshness' and roll it out in the U.S. and the U.K." But when the British saw the ads, they were baffled. "Canned? You mean tinned, right?" They had no idea that what Americans called a 'can,' the Brits referred to as a 'tin.' Mohan quickly learned that words, even in the same language, could mean different things across borders.

Lesson 2: The Colour Conundrum

Next, Sohan designed a sleek, black-and-white packaging for a product launch in Japan. It was minimalist and chic—perfect for the modern consumer.. To his dismay, sales in Japan were dismal. It turns out, black and white in Japan are colours associated with mourning. And when they launched in Hispanic countries, the purple variant didn't do any better. "Who knew purple was the colour of death?" sighed Sohan as he quickly learned that colours carry different meanings in different cultures.

Lesson 3: The Website Whirlwind

Undeterred, they moved on to designing a new website for their Chinese customers. Sohan, a fan of clean and minimal design, filled the site with white space and simple fonts. But Chinese users found it too sparse. "Where's all the information?" they asked. Meanwhile, their European clients loved the simplicity. Sohan couldn't help but laugh, "Who knew white space could be so polarising?"

Lesson 4: The Big Mac Misstep

The duo then ventured into India, where they were tasked with promoting a new line of burgers. "We'll just tweak our classic Big Mac ad," Mohan suggested. But Sohan, wise from their previous blunders, did some quick research. "Hold on,Mohan! Most Indians don't eat beef!" They quickly adapted, launching a chicken and paneer version of the Big Mac, much to the delight of their Indian audience.

Lesson 5: The Cleanliness Conundrum

Mohan, determined to make a splash in the U.S., launched a campaign emphasising cleanliness. "Cleanliness is next to godliness, right?" he quipped. While Americans appreciated the connection between cleanliness and appearance, other cultures saw it differently. "Cleanliness is about health, not looks!" Mohan gently reminded him. *"One man's cleanliness is another man's cultural faux pas."*

Lesson 6: The Time Zone Tangle

One day, they launched a global email campaign. "Let's hit send!" Mohan said, triumphantly pressing the button. But their inboxes soon flooded with angry replies. It turns out, they had sent their emails in the middle of the night in Europe and Asia. "Oops," said Mohan sheepishly, "Next time, let's remember that not everyone's awake when we are."

Lesson 7: The Decision-Making Dilemma

In China, Mohan and Sohan were thrilled to pitch a new product. They prepared a compelling presentation, aimed directly at the CEO. But nothing happened. Puzzled, Mohan discovered that in China, decisions are often made collectively. "We should have provided materials for everyone!" he realised. Sohan added, "And let's not forget that in some places, the oldest person in the room gets the final say."

Lesson 8: The Religious Ruckus

Their next challenge was a holiday campaign. Mohan thought he'd be clever by incorporating some local religious themes. People love it when you reference their traditions! But Sohan, now the wiser of the two, put his foot down. Let's avoid that. It's too easy to get it wrong and offend someone. Mohan nodded in agreement, grateful for the save.

Lesson 9: The Social Structure Surprise

As they expanded into new markets, Mohan and Sohan noticed something odd. Their campaigns were performing differently based on the target audience's social structures. In some places, education and power influence purchasing decisions, Sohan pointed out. We need to research our audience before making assumptions.

Lesson 10: The Motivation Mystery

Finally, they turned their attention to understanding their customers' motivations. B2B clients care about avoiding risks, while B2C customers are driven by personal needs, Mohan observed. Sohan chimed in, We need to address their logical needs, but also appeal to their hidden desires—like convenience or self-esteem.

With each lesson, Mohan and Sohan grew wiser. They learned that going global wasn't just about translating words.

It was about understanding cultures, values, and behaviours.

Their journey was filled with humorous missteps, but each one brought them closer to mastering the art of international marketing.

And so, armed with their newfound knowledge, they launched a series of successful campaigns around the world, proving that with the right insights, you can, indeed, conquer the global market—one cultural nuance at a time.

Moral of the Story

In marketing, especially in international marketing, understanding your audience is half the battle. Clear understanding and appreciation of Cultural and Social Sensitivity is of paramount importance.

In this context quote of David Ogily, the Father of Advertising is quite appropriate when he says:

" The consumer isn't a moron, she is your wife"

By Implication, the quote underscores the importance of understanding your audience deeply and not underestimating their intelligence.

CHAPTER 12

REAL- LIFE CASE STUDIES

Importance of International Marketing for SMEs.

In today's interconnected world, international marketing is no longer a luxury reserved for large corporations.

It's a critical growth strategy for Small and Medium-sized Enterprises (SMEs).

Expanding into global markets offers SMEs a wealth of opportunities, inter alia, including:

- access to larger customer bases
- enhanced brand recognition
- increased competitiveness

However, this journey is not without its share of challenges, sometimes formidable ones at that..

By understanding real-world examples, potential obstacles, and available government support, SMEs can navigate the complexities of international marketing to achieve sustainable growth.

Incorporating Real-World Examples

Case Study 1

Apple: A Global Powerhouse Built on Differentiation and Customer Focus

Apple commands presence in 150 countries.

It enjoyed a staggering revenue of $383.29 billion in 2023.

Apple's success hinges on a brilliant global marketing strategy such as:

Differentiating from Competitors

Apple doesn't chase trends.It sets them. The focus on innovation allows them to create products that stand out. This differentiation strategy has fostered a strong brand identity and a loyal customer base worldwide.

Focusing on Customer

Apple crafts compelling narratives that showcase how iPads revolutionised learning. It places the customer's needs at the centre of the story.

Apple recognises the power of localisation.

Apple tailors marketing messages to resonate with local preferences.

Apple has cultivated a brand synonymous with quality, innovation, and premium craftsmanship.

This reputation attracts customers from all around the globe.

By flawlessly executing this multifaceted marketing strategy, they ensure they'll continue to resonate with consumers as technology evolves.

Case Study 2

Red Bull: Building a Community with Disruptive Brand Storytelling

The iconic slogan and tagline, "Red Bull Gives You Wings" might be catchy. However, the true marketing genius lies in creating a lifestyle association. It owns the space of extreme sports and adventure.

The company leverages strategic sponsorships, event marketing, inspiring content, and innovative media channels. This helped solidify their position as a leader in the energy drinks market and garnered loyalty from consumers worldwide.

The company's brand image is built around the concept of athleisure and adrenaline.

This differentiated the brand from its competitors and helped create consistent messaging that resonated with a thrill-seeking audience worldwide.

Case Study 3

Booking.com: Crushing the Travel Booking Game with Affiliates, Ads, and Reviews

Booking.com is a global leader that has revolutionised how people book accommodations.

It boasts of over 2.7 million properties listed in more than 220 countries and 40 languages.

The success story of Booking.com is based on three pillars:

Global Partnerships: Booking.com leverages a vast affiliate network of travel bloggers, airlines, and other online travel agencies (OTAs). These partners promote Booking.com on their platforms, earning commissions for each referred booking. This network contributes to exponential expansion of Booking.com driving traffic and bookings at minimal upfront cost.

Google Ads: Booking.com has capitalised on the power of Google Ads to capture user intent at the crucial moment – when they're actively searching for travel options. By strategically bidding on relevant keywords like "hotel booking" or "vacation rentals," Booking.com ensures its ads appear at the top of search results, driving high-quality traffic to its website.

Customer Reviews: Booking.com understands the importance of trust and social proof in the travel industry. Their platform allows both guests and property owners to leave reviews, providing transparency to potential guests. Genuine customer reviews on property listings enhance Booking.com's credibility and increase booking confidence.

Case Study 4

Airbnb - Immersive Travel

The online marketplace and hospitality service brokerage company Airbnb is a great example of how to connect people from around the world. Airbnb's UVP, is we allow travellers to find affordable lodging that is more immersive, allowing them to experience new cultures and communities the way they are meant to be.

Airbnb is more than a P2P accommodation provider;

They've built their community by creating trust between users. They encourage regular communication, detailed profiles, and strong reviews. The engagement is phenomenal.

Traveler's of all ages can enjoy an unforgettable experience in a new country with quality lodging — avoiding steep hotel fees and cramped hostels. Meanwhile, hosts can make extra money by renting out the spaces they aren't using.

Creating a sense of community is a sure-fire way to help establish a strong global presence.

Case Study 5

Spotify - Redefining Genre

Spotify has quickly become one of the top music streaming platforms in the world. One of the keys to their success was creating a space for musicians around the world to get exposure to new listeners.

One of the ways they did this was by creating a 'mood' page, where you can find artists and songs based on moods like 'chill,' 'focus,' and 'workout' — as well as traditional genres like 'hip-hop,' 'country,' and 'indie.'

"By changing how they describe their content, Spotify gets users to listen to music that goes beyond their favourite genres and instead satisfies habits and lifestyles that people share all over the world.

Case Study 6

Zoho Corporation

Zoho, an Indian software development company, started as a small enterprise focused on providing affordable software solutions to small businesses. Through strategic international marketing, Zoho expanded its operations globally, now serving over 60 million users across the world.

Zoho's success can be attributed to its understanding of diverse market needs and its ability to localize its products. For instance, Zoho's CRM software offers multi-language support and integrations with region-specific tools, which has helped the company gain a strong foothold in various international markets.

These examples demonstrate how SMEs can achieve remarkable growth by strategically entering international markets, adapting to local needs, and maintaining a consistent brand identity.

PART 10
AN EYE ON FUTURE

"The globalization of markets is at hand. With that, the multinational commercial world nears its end, and so does the multinational marketer."

-*Ted Levitt, Economist and Harvard Business School Professor*

CHAPTER 13

LOOKING AHEAD : EMERGING FUTURE TRENDS

Emerging Trends: Impact of Technology and Globalisation.

The landscape of international marketing is driven by rapid technological advancements. Some new concepts are emerging and gaining traction with each passing day. Understanding these emerging trends is crucial for businesses aiming to stay competitive and leverage new opportunities.

The noteworthy trends shaping the future of international marketing are:

Digital Transformation

Digital transformation is revolutionising:

- engagement of businesses with customers
- streamlining of operations
- driving growth

E-commerce Expansion: Companies are investing in user-friendly online stores, mobile apps, and seamless payment systems to enhance the shopping experience.

Artificial Intelligence (AI) and Machine Learning technologies help businesses understand consumer behaviour, anticipate needs, and deliver tailored experiences.

Big Data and Analytics: The ability to collect and analyse vast amounts of data provides businesses with insights into market trends, customer preferences, and campaign performance. Data-driven decision-making enhances marketing effectiveness and ROI.

Globalisation and Market Expansion

Globalisation continues to break down barriers to international trade, presenting new opportunities for market expansion.

Key trends include:

Emerging Markets: Emerging markets in Asia, Africa, and Latin America are experiencing rapid economic growth and increasing consumer purchasing power. These regions offer significant opportunities for businesses looking to expand their global footprint.

Cross-Border Partnerships: Strategic alliances ,partnerships and collaborations with local businesses facilitate market entry and expansion. They help navigate regulatory environments, cultural differences, and distribution challenges.

Localisation Strategies: Companies are investing in localising products, marketing materials, and customer support to resonate with local audiences and meet regional needs.

Sustainability and Corporate Social Responsibility (CSR): Consumers are increasingly prioritising sustainability and ethical practices in their purchasing decisions.

Key aspects of this trend include:

Sustainable Products: Businesses are developing eco-friendly products and sustainable packaging to meet consumer demand for environmentally responsible choices.

Transparent Supply Chains: Consumers expect transparency in how products are sourced and manufactured.

Businesses are adopting ethical sourcing practices and communicating their CSR initiatives to build trust and loyalty.

Green Marketing: Marketing campaigns highlighting sustainability efforts and eco-friendly products are resonating with environmentally conscious consumers. Green marketing enhances brand reputation and drives customer engagement.

Preparing for the Future: Staying ahead in the rapidly evolving landscape of international marketing requires strategic planning, innovation, and adaptability. In this context, practical strategies for small businesses to pursue for the future are:

Embracing Digital Technologies

Leveraging digital technologies is essential for staying competitive and reaching global audiences.

Key actions include:

Investing in E-commerce: Develop a robust e-commerce platform that offers a seamless shopping experience. Ensure the platform is mobile-friendly, secure, and easy to navigate.

Utilising AI and Automation: Implement AI-driven tools and automation to enhance marketing efforts, customer service, and operational efficiency. This includes chatbots for customer support, AI-powered analytics, and personalised marketing campaigns.

Data-Driven Decision Making: Use data analytics to gain insights into customer behaviour, market trends, and campaign performance. Make informed decisions based on data to optimise marketing strategies and improve ROI.

Expanding into Emerging Markets

Emerging markets present significant growth opportunities for small businesses.

Key strategies in this regard are:

Market Research: Conduct thorough market research to understand the economic conditions, consumer preferences, and competitive landscape of emerging markets. Use this information to identify high-potential opportunities.

Local Partnerships: Form partnerships with local businesses, distributors, and agents who have in-depth knowledge of the market. Local partners can provide valuable insights, facilitate market entry, and help navigate regulatory challenges.

Adapting Products: Customise products to meet the specific needs and preferences of consumers in emerging markets. This may involve modifying product features, packaging, and pricing strategies to align with local tastes and purchasing power.

Focusing on Sustainability

Incorporating sustainability into business practices and marketing strategies is becoming increasingly important.

Key actions include:

Developing Sustainable Products: Invest in research and development to create products that are environmentally friendly and socially responsible. Use sustainable materials, reduce waste, and minimise the carbon footprint.

Communicating CSR Initiatives: Transparently communicate your sustainability efforts and CSR initiatives to consumers. Highlight the positive impact of your practices on the environment and communities.

Engaging in Green Marketing: Create marketing campaigns that emphasise your commitment to sustainability. Use storytelling to share the journey and impact of your sustainable practices, and engage consumers through social media and content marketing.

Expert Insights: It involves opinions and predictions from industry experts.

Wrapping Up

This recipe is enough for equipping your business with tools and insights to excel in the global market place. Every action you take bring your closure to international goals, transforming challenges into milestones.

PART 11
IN HINDSIGHT

"The future of international marketing lies in the ability to connect with people across cultures, creating campaigns that resonate on a personal level while embracing the global context."

- Linda Wolf (Former CEO of Leo Burnett Worldwide)

CHAPTER 14

YOUR KEY TAKEAWAYS

1. Understanding Global Markets

Small businesses must grasp the nuances of different global markets, including cultural, economic, and regulatory factors.

2. Importance of Market Segmentation

Market segmentation allows small businesses to target specific customer groups effectively, enhancing marketing efficiency.

3. Crafting a Winning Marketing Mix

The 4Ps (Product, Price, Place, Promotion) need to be adapted to fit the local preferences and buying behaviours in each target market.

4. Leveraging Digital Marketing

Digital marketing is a cost-effective way for small businesses to reach global audiences, especially through social media, SEO, and content marketing.

5. Effective Distribution Strategies

Efficient distribution is key to making products available in new markets, whether through local partnerships, e-commerce platforms, or direct shipping.

6. Building Strong International Partnerships

Collaborating with local businesses, influencers, and distributors can accelerate market entry and build trust with new customers.

7. Adapting to Legal and Regulatory Requirements

Navigating the legal and regulatory landscape is crucial to avoid pitfalls and ensure compliance in foreign markets.

8. Cultural Sensitivity and Localisation

Cultural differences can significantly impact customer perception and acceptance of your brand.

9. Risk Management

International expansion involves risks such as currency fluctuations, political instability, and supply chain disruptions.

10. Measuring Success

Tracking key performance indicators (KPIs) specific to international markets is essential to gauge success and adjust strategies as needed.

11. Cost-Effective Marketing Campaigns

Small businesses often have limited budgets, so finding creative, cost-effective ways to market internationally is crucial.

12. Long-Term Growth and Scalability

Strategic international marketing should be seen as a long-term investment in the company's growth and scalability.

13. Continuous Learning and Adaptation

The international market landscape is dynamic, requiring ongoing learning and adaptation to remain competitive.

14. Customer-Centric Approach

Understanding and meeting the needs of international customers is the cornerstone of successful global marketing.

15. Building a Global Brand Identity

A strong, consistent brand identity helps small businesses stand out in competitive international markets.

These takeaways encapsulate the essential strategies and actions small businesses should consider when expanding into international markets.

CHAPTER 15
YOUR CHECKLIST FOR ACTION

Marketing Beyond Borders

Preamble

Expanding your small business into international markets is an exhilarating journey brimming with opportunities for unparalleled growth and success. With the right strategy and a meticulously prepared action plan, you can master the complexities of global markets and unlock new frontiers for your business.

This Checklist is designed to be your steadfast guide, ensuring that every step you take is deliberate, precise, and driven by your vision of international triumph.

A Roadmap for SME Businesses

Expanding your small business into international markets is an exciting journey filled with opportunities for growth and success.

With the right strategy and a well-prepared action plan, you can navigate the complexities of global markets and unlock new potential for your business.

This checklist serves as your guide to ensure every step you take is thoughtful, precise, and geared towards achieving international success.

1. **Understanding the Target Market**

    ✅ Conduct market research on the cultural, economic, and legal landscape.

    ✅ Identify local consumer needs and preferences.

2. **Adapting Products and Services**

    ✅ Customise products/services for local tastes and standards.

    ✅ Ensure compliance with local regulations.

3. **Building a Strong Brand Presence**

   ☑ Develop a localised brand message.

   ☑ Engage local influencers and partners.

4. **Effective Digital Marketing**

   ☑ Utilise popular local social media platforms.

   ☑ Implement local SEO strategies.

5. **Establishing Distribution Channels**

   ☑ Choose appropriate distribution channels.

   ☑ Consider local partnerships or e-commerce platforms.

6. **Pricing Strategy**

   ☑ Develop competitive pricing based on local market conditions.

   ☑ Factor in tariffs, shipping, and local taxes.

7. **Cultural Sensitivity and Localization**

   ☑ Respect local customs and traditions in marketing campaigns.

   ☑ Localise content, including language and imagery.

8. **Building Relationships**

    ✅ Network with local businesses and trade associations.

    ✅ Participate in local events and trade shows.

9. **Legal and Regulatory Compliance**

    ✅ Stay informed about local legal and regulatory requirements.

    ✅ Ensure compliance in all business practices.

10. **Monitoring and Evaluation**

    ✅ Regularly monitor marketing performance.

    ✅ Collect customer feedback and adjust strategies.

11. **Risk Management**

    ✅ Identify potential risks in the international market.

    ✅ Develop contingency plans for business continuity.

12. **Market Entry Strategies**

    ✅ Evaluate exporting, franchising, joint ventures, or subsidiaries.

    ✅ Assess each method's pros and cons.

13. Global Branding

☑ Develop a consistent yet flexible global brand strategy.

☑ Register trademarks in international markets.

14. Supply Chain Management

☑ Optimise international logistics.

☑ Ensure cost-effective sourcing, manufacturing, and delivery.

15. Customer Service and Support

☑ Provide multilingual customer support.

☑ Establish local customer service centres or partners.

16. Leveraging Technology

☑ Utilise AI and big data analytics for market insights.

☑ Implement CRM systems for customer relationship management.

17. Financial Planning and Management

☑ Develop a robust financial plan for international operations.

☑ Monitor financial performance and adjust budgets.

18. Intellectual Property Protection

☑ Understand and comply with local IP laws.

☑ Monitor and enforce IP rights.

19. Building Local Teams

☑ Hire local talent for market insights.

☑ Train local teams with company culture and values.

20. Cultural Intelligence

☑ Enhance cultural intelligence within your team.

☑ Conduct cultural sensitivity training.

21. Sustainability and CSR

☑ Adopt sustainable business practices.

☑ Engage in local CSR activities.

22. Continuous Learning and Adaptation

☑ Stay updated with global market trends and technologies.

☑ Pivot and adapt strategies based on feedback and performance.

23. Networking and Partnerships

- ☑ Join international business networks and forums.
- ☑ Collaborate with local businesses and organisations.

24. Legal and Ethical Considerations

- ☑ Understand local ethical standards and business practices.
- ☑ Ensure transparency and ethical conduct.

25. Marketing Mix Adaptation

- ☑ Adjust the 4Ps (Product, Price, Place, Promotion) for local markets.
- ☑ Experiment with different promotional tactics.

26. Customer Experience (CX)

- ☑ Focus on delivering exceptional customer experiences.
- ☑ Gather and analyse customer feedback for continuous improvement.

This checklist can serve as a practical guide to ensure all critical aspects of strategic international marketing are addressed, helping small businesses navigate and succeed in new markets.

By following this checklist, you're equipping your business with the tools and insights needed to thrive in the global marketplace. Each action you take brings you one step closer to realising your international ambitions.

Stay focused, stay committed, and watch your business flourish across borders. The world is ready for what you have to offer—make your mark with confidence.

EPILOGUE

"The future of business is not in isolated markets but in the ability to connect, adapt, and thrive across borders. Success in international marketing is not just about reaching new customers —it's about understanding their world and making your brand indispensable within it."

- *Philip Kotler, Father of Modern Marketing*

IN RETROSPECT

As we conclude this journey of *Marketing Beyond Borders,* let's reflect on the invaluable insights and strategies we've explored. The global marketplace is ever-evolving, filled with opportunities for those ready to embrace change and innovation.

For SMEs, international success may be challenging but incredibly rewarding. This book has shown that with the right mindset and approach—such as understanding cultural nuances, leveraging digital marketing, and staying adaptable—small businesses can thrive on the global stage.

The lessons here go beyond business expansion; they foster a global mindset that values diversity, innovation, and continuous learning. The journey of international marketing is ongoing, with new markets, changing consumer behaviours, and technological advancements creating fresh opportunities.

This marks the end of our exploration. Nonetheless, it is beginning of your global journey. Equipped with the knowledge from these pages, your SME is now poised to reach new heights. The world is your marketplace, and the possibilities are endless.

Thank you for joining me on this journey.
Now, elevate your business to the next level!

A VOTE OF THANKS

A Heartfelt Thank You to My Valued Readers

Dear Valued Reader,

As I sit down to pen this letter, I am filled with gratitude and a myriad of emotions. First and foremost, I want to express my heartfelt thanks to you for taking the time to read my Book.

Your support means the world to me. I am incredibly grateful to have readers like you who invest their precious time and energy into my work. Writing this Book has been a journey of self-discovery, growth, and immense learning.

I sincerely hope that it has touched your life- personal or professional- in some way. It must have ignited your thought process on or around the subject. Your thoughts, feelings, and reactions to this Book are incredibly important. I would be honored if you would share your thoughts by emailing me at vidyut@holis-tique.com

Once again, thank you from the bottom of my heart for your support. I am immensely grateful for the opportunity to share my thoughts and ideas with you. I sincerely hope this Book has brought you some inspiration, purpose and utility.

With deepest gratitude,

Vidyut Shah
Marketing Strategist
Chairman
Holistique Business Consulting Private Ltd.

MARKETING BEYOND BORDERS

A STRATEGIC ROADMAP FOR SME BUSINESSES

SNEAK PEAK OF THE BOOK

- **Understanding International Markets:** Learn the important marketing nuances and marketing research.

- **Crafting an Effective Strategy:** Explore how to tailor-make your marketing- mix to global audience.

- **Navigating Regulations and Trade:** Uncover the complexities of international trade laws.

- **Digital Marketing Across Borders:** Trace the power of digital channels for reaching a global audience.

- **Success Stories of Global Brands:** Get inspired by case studies that have successfully scaled the global plane.

Your Compendium in Odyssey of International Marketing

www.ingramcontent.com/pod-product-compliance
Lightning Source LLC
LaVergne TN
LVHW041916070526
838199LV00051BA/2640